Wisdom is the *Principal* Thing!

Quick Reference Tips for the Pocket of New School Administrators

Dr. Kathy P. Hall

WISDOM IS THE *PRINCIPAL* THING

This book was written, based on the author's personal experiences. The names used in the anecdotes throughout the book have been changed to protect the privacy of individuals. The names of characters, locales, events or incidents that are used in the templates/samples at the end of the book are either a product of the author's imagination or are used in a fictitious manner. To the best of the author's knowledge, all quotations included here fall under the fair use or public domain guidelines of copyright law in the United States, are used by expressed permission of the copyright holder, or are used with the permission of the Copyright Clearance Center.

Published by
Hall's Consulting and Publishing Enterprises 2020
Mountain Island Area, North Carolina
www.hallsconsultingandpublishing.com
ISBN 13: 978-0-9981169-4-5
ISBN 10: 0998116947
Library Control Number: 2018913394

© Copyright 2017 by Dr. Kathy P. Hall
Registration number: (TXu 2-043-637)

Book Credits
Written by Dr. Kathy P. Hall
Edited by Hall's Consulting and Publishing Enterprises
Cover Concept and design by Virtual Illustrations

All rights reserved. Only educators with local school sites or noncommercial or nonprofit entities that have purchased this book are authorized to use the forms and sample documents that are included. Except for that usage, no part of this book may be reproduced or utilized in any form or by any means, electronic or mechanical, including photocopying, recording, or by any information storage and retrieval system, without expressed permission in writing from the publisher, except for the inclusion of brief quotations in a review.

This book is dedicated to my father,
Sergeant George W. Pettice (1925 – 2006),
who taught me this proverb:

Wisdom is the principal thing;
therefore get wisdom: and
with all thy getting, get understanding.

As a military man and as a pastor following retirement, he always emphasized to my siblings and me that while knowledge is important, the application of knowledge is critical for the true understanding of all situations. Indeed, he was the wisest man I have ever known.

Contents

Foreword ix
Preface xi
Acknowledgments xv
Introduction xvii

1: Assemblies 1
2: Audits and Visitations 9
3: "Breathe." 25
4: Communication 35
5: Conferences with Parents 43
6: Conferences with Staff 55
    Members
7: Contacts 63
8: Curriculum 71
9: Diet 83
10: Discipline 91
11: Extended Day Programs 119
12: File Organization 131
13: Handling Emergencies 149
14: Master Scheduling 161
15: New Teacher Support 175
16: Observations and Evaluations 191

vii

17: Opening and Closing the 199
    School Year
18. Prioritizing Responsibilities 215
19: Staff and Volunteer Appreciation 225
20: Supporting Your Supervisor 231
21: Training Coordination 239
22: Twelve Tips for the Wise 255

Final Thoughts 265
End Notes 267
Appendices 271

Letters
A: Assignment to Discipline School 277
B: Notification of Expulsion 279
C: Teacher Recognition 282
D: Student's Accomplishment 284
E: Request for Conference 286
F: Summary of Conference 288

Form Elements and Humor
G: Teacher Observation Form 291
    Elements
H: Find the Humor Anecdotes 295

About the Author 301

FOREWORD

*Wisdom Is the **Principal** Thing* is the first-hand account of a school-based administrator, written in the voice of Dr. Kathy P. Hall and based upon her many field experiences over an extended period of time. In sharing her varied experiences, Dr. Hall provides a quick-reference pathway to addressing problems or predicaments new administrators are sure to confront. Most, if not all, school-based administrative neophytes can benefit from the trial-and-error, field experiences of this successful administrator.

The content of this book is presented in a handy and easy to read fashion. Such is a true benefit for school-based administrators, who seldom have time to read professional text, during the course of a school day. Dr. Hall's presentation style is that of a journalist, via questions and proposed solutions or considerations. Said style is consistent for each topic and throughout the book. While there are some 21 topics to draw from, the list is not exhaustive of the experiences a school-based administrator will be confronted with over time. However, the suggested journalistic approach to reflecting and thus problem-solving may be applied to most any given situation.

Wisdom Is the *Principal* Thing!

For sure, *Wisdom Is the **Principal** Thing*, as Dr. Hall has indicated by way of her title, is only to be followed by Courage and Strength of Character.

Dr. James L. Pughsley,
Retired Superintendent
Charlotte-Mecklenburg Schools
Charlotte, NC

PREFACE

I was a teacher for fifteen years and an assistant principal for eight years at the middle and high school levels. I was promoted and worked as a middle school principal for three years. I then finished my tenure by working at the district office level as an assistant director, responsible for truancy and dropout prevention.

After retiring, I decided to work as a middle school assistant principal in another state for two years. The second year I was there, I got the idea for this book. I thought, "Wow! If I had not come here with my background and experience, the extent of my success in a different state and school district would not have been possible." I thought, "What if I wrote a 'how-to' book for new administrators with great tips about the basics of administration, especially in a school environment?"

If someone had handed this book to me when I first became an administrator, it would have saved me a lot of trials and errors!

So, here it is. I don't have the answer for everything. Working in North Carolina and South Carolina states, each has very different laws, requirements and populations of teachers and students. However, after 38 years in education, here is what I do know.

Wisdom Is the *Principal* Thing!

Although each school, each district, and each state are very different from the other, there are common threads of effective administration that run through every educational entity. New administrators need a handy tool to help expedite a smooth transition from the classroom to the administrative team. This book will allow brand new administrators to hold a small book that contains information they can implement, step by step, *immediately*. Contrary to many administrative books that are full of data, philosophy, and theories about student assessment, instructional techniques, pedagogy, school climate, and much needed teacher development, this "how-to" book fits into a pocket and can be carried anywhere.

Topics range in *alphabetical order* from how to prioritize and organize; how to prepare for audits, visits, and assemblies; how to coordinate curriculum and instruction, extended day programs, and opening and closing of school and how to effectively communicate with everyone. Other important areas include effective student discipline strategies as well as effective parent and staff member conferences. This tool will walk you through how to handle emergency situations and how to coordinate trainings, master scheduling, new teacher support, and staff appreciation. You will be taught how to keep your cool in a chapter entitled "Breathe," and elements of

Preface

an observation form for teachers plus tips and templates of letters for a variety of purposes are included. This book can be used for training new school administrators, used for a textbook for coursework in school administration, and used for preparing candidates for administrative interviews and principal internships.

You, who are principals, as the middle person between district level personnel and school constituents, can place this pocket full of wisdom in the hands of your new administrators, knowing that they will have step-by-step instructions on how to approach many responsibilities. You will watch them quickly and successfully complete their duties and begin to embrace the opportunities to grow in instructional leadership and other areas that are key to becoming an effective, future school principal.

You, who are assistants, whether your title is Dean, Assistant Principal, Vice Principal, Director or Lead Teacher, must aid your principal with these responsibilities in a variety of publics. So, use wisdom. You can begin by applying the principles of this book, which first teaches you how to apply the journalists' questions to *any* school situation. You will learn how to effectively address all situations with the organizational thought process demonstrated in this book. You will also possess specific steps that will

Wisdom Is the *Principal* Thing!

guide you on implementing twenty-one categories of administrative duties, not including the tips and the appendices.

Use this book and watch your work life become much more manageable! You can tweak, enhance, add or delete, according to the needs of your students, staff, parents, school, and community. That's using wisdom too!

ACKNOWLEDGMENTS

I offer many thanks to James L. Pughsley, Donna Parker-Tate, Beverly G. Logan, and Patricia Jackson for their input on this project. I also thank Cynthia Butler King, Cheryl Foard, and Laverda Jessamy Dinkins, who have always supported me and encouraged me to reach my goals.

I appreciate my principals who afforded me many opportunities to grow into an effective leader. I thank my former co-workers and awesome *GCABSE* colleagues, who worked with me tirelessly for many years to make the world a better place for children. I am grateful for my friends and family members who believed in me and supported my endeavors, even during my moments of doubt, especially my mother, Catherine Pettice, and my husband, Trent P. Hall.

INTRODUCTION

After retiring from public education, I was contracted to teach writing and research methods to freshman students at a community college. One of the most effective pre-writing strategies that I taught students to use noted the six main questions to ask, concerning any situation. I did not invent this concept. Not only is it a great pre-writing strategy that I used as an English teacher and an author, but journalists have been using these questions as the backbone of their interviewing and reporting plans for years.

The who, what, when, where, why, and how of a situation gives at least a beginning structure to *any* task you may encounter. I was in a class once, and the instructor gave us an assignment with no directions at all. The assignment was for us to form twelve topics on a particular subject, to discuss and explain the topics, and to make a notebook with this information. The notebooks would be due by a certain date to be graded, of course. The students in the class were confused, stressed and freaking out. Many expressed, not to the teacher, of course, that they didn't appreciate not being told *how* to do the assignment and not being given any specifics about expectations. Immediately, I thought of the journalists' questions. I chose the subject, discussed the who,

Wisdom Is the *Principal* Thing!

what, when, where, why, and how of each topic, and sectioned my notebook, accordingly, with dividers. I made an "A."

I cannot tell you how many times a situation would come up, as a new administrator, when I was not sure how to approach a particular assignment. I would start with the journalists' questions, and the tasks would develop structure and organization. The journalists' questions, which are applied in this alphabetically organized book, have checklists of most of the typical administrative duties that can save you, as a new administrator, much time and frustration. Make these questions yours. It's a simple but effective technique!

Use Your Journalists' Questions!

1. **Who** needs to be involved in this task?
    - Who needs to work on it?
    - Who needs to be informed about it?
    - Who will be impacted by it?

2. **What** is the content of the task?
    - What is the issue?
    - What are the concerns?
    - What needs to be done?

Introduction

3. **When** will the task occur?
    - Dates
    - Times

4. **Where** will the task be held? Location?
    - Address
    - Building
    - Office
    - Room or suite

5. **Why** is the task being planned?
    - What is the purpose?
        - Action required
        - Information session
        - Planning session
        - Training session
    - What is the desired outcome?
        - Growth of performance for faculty members and students
        - Improvements in school programs, assessment results, or communications
        - Preparedness for pending audits, visits, meetings, trainings, or the opening and closing of the school year

Wisdom Is the *Principal* Thing!

- Settlements of disputes concerning staff members, students, or parents

6. **How** will the task be structured?
    - How long will it take?
    - How much will it cost?
    - How will you communicate it?
    - How will you decide what is to happen, 1st, 2nd, 3rd, and so on?
    - How long do you have to complete it?
        - Days
        - End of quarter or semester
        - Months
        - Sessions
        - School year

If you need to research something that has already occurred, you can still use the *same questions with the past tense!*

Application of the Journalists' Questions

Your journalists' questions can apply to anything, as the subsequent chapters will demonstrate, but consider the following possibilities:

1. Activities

Introduction

- Assemblies
- Fundraisers
- PTA/PTO Meetings

2. Audits and visitations
   - Accreditation
   - Awards and recognitions
   - Exceptional Children
   - Financial
   - Health
   - Safety
   - Testing

3. Conferences
   - Community personnel
   - District personnel
   - Parent and student
   - Staff member

4. Curricular
   - Assemblies for awards and recognitions
   - Effective instruction
   - Extended day programs

5. Emergencies
   - Active shooter drills

Wisdom Is the *Principal* Thing!

- Fire and tornado drills
- Early dismissals or school closings
- Emergency lockdown procedures

6. Extra-Curricular activities
   - Athletics
   - Clubs and organizations
   - Competitions
   - Concerts and drama performances

7. Meetings you coordinate
   - Committee
   - Department or grade level
   - Special areas - Exceptional Children or English Language Learners (ELL)
   - Staff
   - Team

8. Opening and closing school
   - Handbooks
   - Materials and equipment
   - Orientations
   - Procedures

9. Schedules
   - Master schedule of classes with student and teacher assignments

Introduction

- Testing

10. Student discipline
    - Counselor/Social Worker sessions
    - Mediations
    - Time outs and In-School suspensions
    - Out-of-school suspensions
    - Exclusions/Expulsions

11. Teacher observations and evaluations
    - Formal
    - Informal

12. Trainings and workshops
    - Community
    - Parents
    - Staff members
    - Students

I have been able to bring wisdom and understanding to the issue or task at hand and execute duties with precision and clarity to all of those involved by thoroughly answering these six journalists' questions. You will see how it can be done, and you will, certainly, do it too.

CHAPTER 1

ASSEMBLIES

Assemblies are a necessary part of school life, especially as students become older. It is best to plan well and to be proactive. There is always the risk of things getting out of hand when students are assembled into large groups.

During my first three years as an assistant principal, I was placed in charge of fundraising. One year, I planned a fundraising assembly with the representative of the company, so everyone could be on the same page. This was a middle school, so I cautioned him, saying that middle schoolers are excitable, so while we want them to be excited enough to sell the product, things would need to stay orderly, and he would need to *proceed with caution*.

The representative gave his presentation, and at the end, he got a box of candy and started throwing small bags of candy to the audience. Just imagine middle school kids jumping up to catch the candy and clamoring all over one another. Oh, *my goodness*! For a moment, there was chaos and danger. I had to take a big breath, go calmly, straight to the representative, and order him to *stop throwing candy*. He did stop, and we got the kids settled enough to

Wisdom Is the *Principal* Thing!

finish the assembly and get them back into their classes. I was so grateful no one was hurt and a fight didn't break out! However, even though I knew that *he knew* what he was doing, I had not been specific enough, when I told him we wanted the students to be excited about the fundraiser, but the assembly needed to be orderly. So, when it comes to assemblies, prepare carefully, implement wisely, and follow through. Additionally, without a doubt, it helps to be *specific*.

PREPARATION

Use Your Journalists' Questions!

1. **Who** will be required to come to the assembly?
   Who will be invited to come?
   Who will coordinate it (opening/closing)?
   Who will present?

2. **What** will be the content of the assembly?
   What information needs to be disseminated?
   - Competitions, spelling bees, debates
   - Fundraising
   - Informational (discipline or graduation requirements)
   - Motivational (guest speakers)

Assemblies

- Performances: band, chorus, orchestra, theatre presentations, and guest artists
- Testing plans or issues

What materials, furniture and/or other items will be needed?

- Awards and certificates
- Audio-Visuals
  - Overhead projector/LCD
  - PowerPoint capabilities
  - Screen
  - Technology Accessibilities
    - Computer
    - Software
    - Smart Board
- Handouts/Evaluation tools
- Refreshments
- Tables and seats

3. **When** will it be conducted?
   - Date
   - Time

   When will it begin and when will it end?
   - One hour
   - Two hours
   - Three hours (Graduation rehearsal)

Wisdom Is the *Principal* Thing!

4. **Where** at the school will it be held? Capacity? Handicapped accessibility? Transportation needs?
   - Auditorium
   - Cafeteria
   - Gym
   - Media Center
   - Multi-purpose room

   Where at another location will it be held? Capacity? Handicapped accessibility? Transportation needs?
   - Another city
   - Another school
   - Another building
     - Building number
     - Floor number
     - Suite or room number

5. **Why** is the assembly being conducted?
   - Goal
   - Purpose

   Why is the state or district requiring it?
   Why does the school need to have it?

6. **How** will the assembly be structured?
   - Things allowed or not allowed
   - Participant involvement
     - Group work

Assemblies

- Lectures
- Moving around
- Sitting down
- Participant seat assignments
  - Classes
  - Departments or grade levels
  - Lunch schedules
  - Teams

How will presenters be recruited?
- In-house resources
- Outside resources

How will presenters be compensated?
- Gifts
- Stipends
- Contract/budget allotments

How will the food be purchased?

How will you notify those you are *requiring* to attend?

How will you notify those you are *inviting* to attend?

IMPLEMENTATION

1. Have the area set up with furniture, including a podium and other décor such as plants.
2. Have needed technology and audio visuals in place.

Wisdom Is the *Principal* Thing!

3. Have required assemblies during the morning, if possible. It's calmer. Fun, excitable assemblies can be in the afternoon, just before dismissal.
4. Notify teachers and other staff members, whether they are directly involved or not. Give no less than a two-week's notice.
5. Communicate the following to all:
    - Arrival and dismissal times
    - Entry times by classrooms, grade levels, halls, departments, buildings, and so on. Do *not* have students to come from lunch or from outside.
    - Duty stations that are assigned during arrival, dismissal and assembly times
    - Emergency exit procedures
    - Transportation details, if applicable
6. Remind teachers to collect permission slips, as needed, and to review appropriate assembly behavior with students, beforehand.
    - Do not call out
    - Do not make fun of or boo others
    - Sit still, pay attention, and clap at appropriate times
7. Make sure the guests, especially visitors who may not be familiar with the school rules, are informed about everything before assembly times.

Assemblies

8. Have students to leave from a class, preferably escorted by a staff member, to come to an assembly. If not, they will be excited, and *without* proper supervision, there will be a potential for problems. Consider the age of students.
9. Assign key personnel to a group of students to help.
    - Assistant principals
    - Counselors
    - Itinerant staff members
    - Security personnel
    - Teachers and teacher assistants
10. File students in orderly and fill in all of the seats. Instruct them to leave no empty seats. A student climbing over another to sit in an empty seat can trigger a conflict.
11. Give the purpose of the assembly.
12. Watch the students carefully during the assembly.
13. Do not give out handouts or programs during the assembly unless the students are attending a senior high school. They will end up left on the seats, or in the isles, hallways, restrooms, and trashcans. It is best to have the teachers to give them out when they return to the classroom.

Wisdom Is the *Principal* Thing!

FOLLOW-THROUGH

1. Depending on how students are seated, dismiss by a staggered schedule as follows:
    - Departments or grade levels
    - Rows
    - Teacher class assignments
    - Teams
2. Have school personnel posted in key locations while students are transitioning to classes, other assigned areas, or transportation points.
3. Set a time for all students to be back in their classrooms, in other assigned areas, or at transportation points.
4. Let the students and teachers know the success of the assembly. Give congratulations for good behavior.

You cannot predict everything that will happen when you are working with large groups of students, but you can, at least, plan and anticipate as much as possible.

To hope for the best and prepare for the worst, is a trite but a good maxim.

John Jay

CHAPTER 2

AUDITS AND VISITATIONS

AUDITS

Audits can be scary! There are many different types of audits, and I think auditors don't feel they have done their jobs unless they find *something* wrong! This does not have to reflect badly on you or the rest of the administrative team. My experiences with auditors have found that as long as there are only a few irregularities, they will allow you a certain amount of time to address the errors, and they will come back to make sure the errors have been corrected. Just don't make the mistake of *not* correcting the errors cited. No excuses. If they find too many irregularities or issues, they might threaten to close the school. Guess what? They have the authority to do just that, especially if health, safety, or federal guidelines are at stake. Now that you know this, you can focus on what you need to do to be prepared.

PREPARATION

Use Your Journalists' Questions!

Wisdom Is the *Principal* Thing!

1. **Who** is coming to do the audit?
    - County or local officials
    - District officials
    - Federal officials
    - State officials

    Who needs to be designated to be involved in the preparation for and the execution of the audit?
    - Assistant Principal
    - Cafeteria Manager
    - Curriculum Facilitator
    - Department Chairperson
    - Grade Level Chairperson
    - Secretary (financial/records)
    - Head Custodian
    - Media Specialist
    - School Nurse
    - School security and school resource officer
    - Teacher of children with special needs
    - Team Leader
    - Technology Coordinator

2. **What** kind of audit is it?
    - Academic Records
        - Exceptional and Gifted children

Audits and Visitations

- English Language Learners
> Curriculum delivery
- District classroom observers
- State classroom observers
> Cafeteria and Food Services
> Financial
> Follow-up audits: Errors and inconsistencies were found, and they came back to check corrective measures.
> Health procedures
> Inventory of equipment and furniture
> Maintenance
> Media (audio and visual)
> Operational: how efficiently you conduct fire drills or tornado drills
> Safety
> Technology
> Testing

3. **When** will the audit occur?
    > Date
    > Time

4. **Where** will the audit be held? Location?
    > Cafeteria
    > Classrooms

Wisdom Is the *Principal* Thing!

- Equipment rooms
- Gym
- Hallways
- Health room
- Media Center
- Offices
- Outside areas
- Storage areas
- Transportation areas (bus lot, parent drop-off/pick-up lane)

5. **Why** is the audit being planned? The purpose?
    - Per guidelines
        - Federal audit
        - District audit
        - State audit
    - Routine audit
    - Targeted audit as a result of complaints or noted inconsistencies

6. **How** will the audit be structured?
    - During *before* and *after school* times
    - During break times
    - During class times
    - During lunch times

    How will you anticipate their wishes?

Audits and Visitations

- Will there be tasty snacks, hot coffee, or cold drinks for the auditors?
- Will they expect records to be pulled and given to them to audit?
- Will they walk around and look?
- Will they sit in classes?

IMPLEMENTATION

Expected Audits

1. Review regulations for the targeted areas. Include all pertinent personnel.
2. Free personnel up, if at all possible, to help prepare.
3. Make sure your supervisor knows about the audit if he or she has not already been informed.
4. Check and double-check the areas being audited. There may be irregularities that you can address before the audit.
5. Have personnel available to give the auditor a map, a place to work, an escort, if needed, and answers to questions. Even if auditors have a map, make certain that they know where the adult restrooms are located.

Wisdom Is the *Principal* Thing!

6. Make sure all involved personnel are prepared to address questions, sensibly, and not say, "I don't know," or get defensive. This can raise even more questions or can make it appear as if they are negligent or have something to hide. I tried to make sure the person over that area of responsibility was available to talk with the auditor.
7. Make sure involved personnel are prepared with a plan of attack if irregularities are cited: "Mr. Clean is our head custodian, and I will make sure he finds another place to secure the vacuum cleaner during class changes, so no student will be hurt."
8. Do *not* make excuses. They do *not* want to hear them!
9. Be ready to tell the auditor exactly what will be done to correct the issue.

Unexpected Audits

Prepare for audits all year whether you have been advised of a coming audit or not. As a result, you will always be ready. Surprise or unexpected audits will occur, but there will be fewer irregularities cited, if you are always ready because you put the *same*

Audits and Visitations

things in place as you would for an expected audit! Run your school like you *know* you will be audited tomorrow!

FOLLOW-THROUGH

1. Study the audit report very carefully.
2. Formulate ideas for implementing corrective measures.
3. Meet and share the report with the people who are responsible for that area.
4. Get input and suggestions from all of the responsible persons.
5. Encourage all participants in the meeting to come to a consensus, concerning the best way to address corrective measures.
6. Notify your immediate supervisor and the key personnel in the superintendent's office concerning the results, so they will not be blindsided by questions. Give the plans for correcting the issues noted in the report.
7. Decide with your immediate supervisor if anyone else needs to be informed such as parents and community personnel. This should depend upon the nature of the audit. For example, a financial audit would not need to be discussed

with the parents or community; however, if a health audit shows results of possible dangers to health and/or an ultimatum has been given for closing the school, you would want to be prepared to contact parents and issue a statement to the community.
8. Implement, immediately and thoroughly, the corrective measures that are needed.
9. Be prepared for a surprise audit to see if corrective measures are in place.

VISITATIONS

Visitations can be scary too! The good thing about visitations is they can bring positive recognition to your school, which can impact its image and its evaluation for awards. When my school first opened, I received requests from parents who wanted to visit to make decisions concerning our school and see if our school was the place for their children. I received many requests from business personnel who wanted to consider partnering with the school for mentoring and tutoring programs. It was a partial magnet, and other schools' personnel visited to see programs such as our after-school program because our school was the first to implement after school childcare for middle school children. Sure, there is a certain amount of nervousness that comes with the desire to put your best foot forward, figuratively speaking; however, if you consider all of the elements involved and prepare, you will become an expert at preparing for multiple kinds of visitations.

PREPARATION

Use Your Journalists' Questions!

1. **Who** is coming to visit the school?
    - Visitors from other schools in your district
    - Visitors from other districts in your state
    - Visitors from districts in other states
    - Visitors from other countries
    - Visitors from the community such as people from educational programs and businesses

    Who needs to be involved in the preparation for and execution of the visitation?
    - Assistant Principal
    - Academic Facilitator
    - Cafeteria Manager

Wisdom Is the *Principal* Thing!

- Department Chairperson
- Secretary (financial/records)
- Head Custodian
- Media Specialist
- School Nurse
- Security personnel or school resource officer
- Teachers
- Technology Coordinator

2. **What** kind of visitation is it?
    - Accreditation
    - Evaluation
    - Media recognition

3. **When** will the visitation occur?
    - Date
    - Time

4. **Where** will the visitation occur? Location?
    - Classrooms
    - Entire school building
    - Special areas
        - Cafeteria
        - Gym
        - Media Center

Audits and Visitations

- Offices
- Technology and other labs
➢ Outside areas
- Athletic and other fields
- Playgrounds
➢ Transportation areas
- Bus lot
- Parent drop-off/pick-up lane

5. **Why** are the visitors coming?
   ➢ Demonstration of quality in certain areas:
   - School operations
   - Instructional excellence
   - Parent involvement, community involvement, or both
   - Student-centered programs
   ➢ Prerequisite for state/national awards
   ➢ Recommended by federal, state, or district personnel for duplication

6. **How** will the visit be structured?
   ➢ Will it be coordinated and led by district-level administrators? Will they do the following?
   - Be escorted by school personnel

Wisdom Is the *Principal* Thing!

- Review documentation
- Structure visitation times
- Talk to parents and students
- Talk to staff members
- View specific programs or special curricular implementations

IMPLEMENTATION

Expected Visitations

1. Include all pertinent personnel.
2. Free personnel up to help prepare.
3. Double-check the areas that visitors are likely to visit. There may be issues that need attention before the visit.
4. Have personnel available to give the visitors a map, escort them, and answer their questions.
5. Make sure pertinent personnel are prepared to address questions, sensibly and amiably. As I did with audits, I made sure the person over that area of responsibility was available to talk with the visitors.
6. Inform your supervisor as a courtesy. He or she may want to drop by to meet the visitors.

Audits and Visitations

7. Inform students and parents if dignitaries from the state, other states, federal departments, or other countries are coming.
8. Do *not* make excuses. Visitors do *not* want to hear them! Put your best foot forward and let them draw their own conclusions.
9. Be ready to invite them to a reception area where amenities are offered such as coffee and snacks, where they can hang their hats and coats, and where they can leave their briefcases, etc. Allow them time to partake of the amenities. Make sure that they know where the adult restrooms are located. If possible, make sure the restrooms are within proximity to the reception area.

Unexpected Visitations

Implement the same elements as those of an expected visit, whether you have been advised of a coming visit or not. Surprise or unexpected visits will occur, especially if your school is outstanding with many awards/recognitions. District office personnel like to show their good schools and will recommend your school for visitations. If you put the *same things* in place as you would for an expected visitation, you will always be ready, as a result. Run your school like you know you can have a visitor at any time!

FOLLOW-THROUGH

1. Pay attention to what the visitors say about your school, receive accolades and constructive criticisms, cheerfully, and use the information to not only improve but to also maintain your school's reputation.
2. Formulate ideas for implementing up-grades, if needed.
3. Meet and share the report with the people responsible for the highlighted areas.
4. Get input from the responsible persons, especially, if improvements are needed.
5. Come to a consensus concerning the best way to implement improvement measures.
6. Notify your immediate supervisor and personnel in the superintendent's office, concerning the results of the visit, so they won't be blindsided by any questions or comments. Give the plans for improvements, if there is constructive criticism.
7. Decide with your supervisor if anyone else needs to be informed of the visit such as par-

Audits and Visitations

ents, media and/or community personnel. This should depend upon the nature of the visit. For example, visitors from another school would not need to be discussed with the parents or the community; however, if visitors come from other districts, other states, federal departments or other countries, you will want to be prepared to inform parents and community personnel.
8. Implement, immediately and thoroughly, any improvement measures that are needed.
9. Inform staff members, students, and parents about the positive comments made about the school. This will encourage them and you too!

He who fails to plan is planning to fail.

Anonymous

CHAPTER 3

"BREATHE."

I cannot tell you how important it is to find a way to calm yourself down in times of emergencies, attacks, and simultaneous challenges. I have seen administrators, new and experienced, who would somehow lose it, only to hurt their staff members, alienate parents, anger district personnel, and negatively impact students.

No matter the amount of education, amount of experience, or importance of position, we must learn strategies for getting the job done without taking things personally and without damaging relationships. I have seen teachers berated and blamed for things that were not their fault. I have seen parents leave the school, unnecessarily angered to the point of removing the child from the school, contacting the school board members, and even contacting the media. I say "unnecessarily" because the situations could have been handled so much more effectively to the benefit of all, especially the child.

When situations become difficult, the true character of a person is revealed. That's when you really see character traits that you may not have seen before. Some administrators lie, some blame it on others,

Wisdom Is the *Principal* Thing!

and some unleash their frustrations on others. Some say mean-spirited things and react with resentment and vindictiveness. Some become angry, use profanity, and act unprofessional in other ways because they just don't know what else to do at the moment. That's when I say, "Breathe."

PREPARATION

Use Your Journalists' Questions!

1. ***Who*** needs to breathe?
   - ➤ You
   - ➤ Everyone else involved

2. **What** do you need to do to breathe?
   - ➤ Take a time-out.
   - ➤ Breathe slowly.
   - ➤ Calm down by thinking of something positive.

3. **When** do you need to breathe?
   - ➤ When you feel angry
   - ➤ When you feel stressed out
   - ➤ When you feel confused
   - ➤ When you feel fearful

"Breathe."

- ➢ When you feel overwhelmed from the culmination of too many things at once
- ➢ When you feel you are at the point of losing control of what you are about to think, say and do

4. **Where** do you need to breathe?
   - ➢ A corner or nook
   - ➢ A restroom
   - ➢ An office
   - ➢ A room or classroom
   - ➢ A storage room
   - ➢ An outside area
   - ➢ Anywhere you can find *privacy*

5. **Why** do you need to breathe?
   - ➢ To maintain professionalism
   - ➢ To have time to think about the next step
   - ➢ To slow your heart rate down
   - ➢ To calm your mind and your spirit
   - ➢ To refrain from thinking and then doing or saying something you may later regret

6. **How** do you breathe?

Wisdom Is the *Principal* Thing!

- ➤ You first breathe in slowly through your nose for about four seconds.
- ➤ You then breathe out slowly through your mouth for five to eight seconds.

IMPLEMENTATION

Use Breathing Techniques for Effectiveness

Breathing techniques slow my heart rate, clear my head, and definitely, lower my stress level. Once I calm down, my productivity increases because I can think with more clarity, which leads to greater learning capacity and much better decision-making. Do you remember those exams, speeches, and presentations in college? Do you remember a time when your students' behavior in the classroom made you or almost made you lose it? I am sure you took deep breaths to calm yourself down.

We do not like to talk about it, but educators have fears too. Breathing helps with fear. Administrators, especially, fear the loss of control *of* situations.

New administrators who were experts at controlling classroom situations often make the mistake of thinking the expertise *automatically* transfers to the whole school level. Not so. So, when things hit you

"Breathe."

like a ton of bricks, and your heart rate and stress levels start to rise, *"**Breathe**."*

1. **Take time *out* to breathe.**
   - Take long, slow, deep breaths.
   - Count until you are calm.
   - Read something.
   - Sing or hum a song or listen to *your* song on your phone for a moment or two.
   - Get a squeeze ball and squeeze it.
   - Pray or meditate.
   - Do brief stretches or exercises.
   - Stretch, scrunch, or wiggle your toes
   - Massage your ear lobes or scalp
   - Find balance.
   - Find your center.
   - Find your faith.
   - Find your peace.
   - Recite your mantra: that statement which always reminds you of who you are, what's really important, and what you are trying to do as a whole.
   - Remind yourself that it's *not* about you. It's about what is *best* for all kids.

Wisdom Is the *Principal* Thing!

When you take time to breathe, you will be surprised how creative you can be at coming up with professional solutions. I have done this and actually gotten great ideas. I returned to the situation with something to say that just popped into my mind, once I calmed down! There were also times when the persons involved in the situation had time to calm down also, and to my surprise, they apologized to me!

2. Go Away to Breathe.

- Go to visit family members or friends whom you haven't seen for a while.
- Take mini getaways.
- Take vacations.

3. Take Time Off to Breathe.

Taking time off and going on vacations will help you to breathe too! Build these moments into your schedule when you can. You should have your principal's permission, so all aspects of school operations can continue to run smoothly while you are gone.

One year, I worked extremely hard on the master schedule all summer. It was a monumental task because we had 1,250 students registered, many whose parents had registered them late. It was about two

"Breathe."

weeks before school was set to start, and I was stressed out! I had worked days and nights through out the weeks, worked on Saturdays, and worked on Sunday afternoons and evenings.

A district administrator called to check on me. During the conversation, he asked me if I had taken a vacation. I told him I had not because I did not have the time. He told me, "Kathy, you need to get away from it for at least a couple of days. If you don't, you will be no good to anyone. Go away for a couple of days, and when you come back, you will be refreshed, and you will have a better perspective." So, reluctantly, I did. My husband and I went away to the mountains for the weekend, without the children. My colleague was right. I came back renewed and ready to go.

The master schedule was completed on time, and all of the students who were registered had their schedules when they reported to school the first day. Find a way to take some time off.

- Go out with friends.
- Go to see a theatrical performance or a great movie.
- Go on a tour of a historical location, a museum or a gallery.
- Take long baths with fragrances.
- Get in a jacuzzi or get a massage.

Wisdom Is the *Principal* Thing!

- ➤ Go for a swim.
- ➤ Go exercise.
- ➤ Go shopping. Don't spend *too* much.
- ➤ Go for long walks, or ride a bike.
- ➤ Go to a salon or barbershop and get a new look. Keep it professional.
- ➤ Volunteer to do something thoughtful and neat for someone who is not as blessed as you are.
- ➤ Take a class or learn to do something *new* in the area of *your* passion.

FOLLOW-THROUGH

1. Return to the situation that made you need to breathe.
2. Have an open mind to some things you may not have wanted to entertain before.
3. Make more of an effort to put yourself in the other person's place.
4. Consider a consensus, as long as it is not non-negotiable such as criminal, abusive, or neglectful.
5. Come to a resolution of the issue.
6. Don't take the frustration home with you. Breathe just before you walk through the door of your home. Remember, your family does not

"Breathe."

deserve your unleashing of frustration on them. My family helped me by giving me 15 minutes to get in the door, put my briefcase down, and sit and unwind before they told me about their day. Believe it or not, that 15 minutes made a *world* of difference with my attitude and approach!

"**Breathe**." You must do this, administrators. It will save your life and, possibly, your job!

The ultimate measure of a man is not where he stands in moments of comfort and convenience, but where he stands at times of challenge and controversy.

Martin Luther King, Jr.

CHAPTER 4

COMMUNICATION

You must decide which type of communication is the best fit for the task you have to accomplish. For example, if you need to inform your faculty members about the new testing procedures, you will need to have the new procedures in writing, and you will need to have an information or training session for all staff members who will be involved. An information or training session will give everyone an opportunity to ask questions and have input, and the written format will allow them to refer to the procedures for review. Whatever you do, communication is the key. Decide how you will communicate the information you need to give or receive from your staff, parents, community, and professional contacts.

PREPARATION

Use Your Journalists' Questions!

1. **Who** will need to be involved in the task?
    - Colleagues
    - Community personnel

Wisdom Is the *Principal* Thing!

- District level personnel
- Federal or state personnel
- Parents
- Staff members

2. **What** do they do?
   What are their areas of responsibilities?
   - Committee chairpersons
   - Department chairpersons
   - District personnel
   - Team leaders
   - Community organization presidents
   - School liaisons

3. **When** are they available?
   When will you need them to be in place?
   - Date
   - Time

4. **Where** will the tasks occur?
   Where do you need them to be?
   - Classroom
   - Community facility
   - Gym
   - Media Center
   - Multipurpose Room
   - Office

Communication

- School grounds

5. **Why** do you need to communicate with them?
    - To aid you in doing a task
    - To complete a task for you
    - To distribute information to them
    - To obtain feedback

6. **How** can you contact them?
    - Cell phone
    - Courier
    - Email
    - Face-to-Face
    - Postal mail
    - Office phone or fax
    - Staff mailboxes

    How can they best help you to do your job?

IMPLEMENTATION

1. Communicate with staff members through a variety of venues, effectively.
    - Emails
    - Face-to-face chats
    - Information sessions
    - Intercom announcements
    - Letters

Wisdom Is the *Principal* Thing!

- Meetings/Conferences
- Memos and handouts
- Telephone calls – automated or conference
- Texts
- Radios for the administrators, secretaries and security personnel only
- Workshops or trainings

2. Communicate with parents through a variety of venues, effectively.
    - Banners/ Signs
    - Brochures
    - Conferences
    - Emails
    - Fliers
    - Information sessions
    - Letters
    - Marquees
    - Meetings with groups or individuals
    - Memos
    - Newsletters/Newspapers (school)
    - Newspapers (community)
    - Social Media/School Websites
    - Telephone calls (automated and conference)
    - Workshops

Communication

- Yearbooks/Annuals

3. Communicate with the community through a variety of venues, effectively.
    - Banners/Signs
    - Brochures
    - Conferences
    - Emails
    - Fliers
    - Information sessions
    - Letters
    - Marquees
    - Meetings
        - School Board
        - Parent/Teacher Association
        - Home Owners' Association
        - Housing Authority
        - Charity Organizations
        - Business Groups
        - Mentoring/Tutoring Groups
    - Memos
    - Newsletters/Newspapers (school)
    - Newspapers (community)
    - Podcasts
    - Social media/Websites
    - Television

Wisdom Is the *Principal* Thing!

- ➢ Telephone calls (automated or conference)
- ➢ Workshops

4. Communicate effectively, generally, by using these final tips.
    - ➢ Memos and letters should be sent in a timely manner.
    - ➢ Progress reports for every student should be sent regularly and in time for the student to improve.
    - ➢ Fliers and brochures should be visible and available.
    - ➢ Marquees, signs, banners, and websites should be current and *never* old news.
    - ➢ Newsletters and newspapers should be consistently sent, so the families and community personnel will know when to expect them.
    - ➢ All communication channels, including yearbooks, should be as error free as possible.
    - ➢ Presentations and information sessions should include clarity of speech and enough time for questions. In all

Communication

communications, especially conferences, do the following:
- Think before you speak.
- Make sure you take the time to understand what the people are trying to convey. Ask questions and summarize what they say. If they indicate that you are being condescending, tell them that you just want to make *sure* you have heard them correctly and understand what they want or need.

FOLLOW-THROUGH

1. Emails and telephone calls should receive a response within 24 – 48 hours. Within 24 hours is *highly* recommended. Letters and notes should receive an acknowledgment of receipt within 24 – 48 hours, depending upon whether they are delivered or mailed. Your acknowledgment should also always include your timeline for giving a response.
2. Communicate, with a *calm* tone, the facts, not hearsay.

Wisdom Is the *Principal* Thing!

3. Communicate only what you know. Do not assume or take a wild guess. Do not even take a so-called "educated guess"!
4. Critical verbal conversations should always be followed up with written communications: For example, disciplinary actions for staff members and students.
5. Be well spoken. Communicate precisely with *tact* and clarity.
6. Do what you *say* you will do! You are only as good as your word.

It is essential to build an effective list of *contacts* with whom you need to communicate, whether they are over departments or are working within departments. Know who is necessary for and will be helpful in aiding you to carry out your responsibilities. See more information on contacts in Chapter 7.

Communications, or the ability to inform people what you expect of them in understandable terms and the ability to transmit to them your interest in them, is the key to successful leadership.

General Harold K. Johnson

CHAPTER 5

CONFERENCES WITH PARENTS

You will deal with parents who are in control of their households and children, and you will deal with parents whose children are running the households. You will deal with parents who are supportive of the school and its goals, and you will deal with parents who could care less about the school or others and are only concerned about their children's happiness. Parents can be your greatest fans, or they can be your greatest nightmare.

My very first year as an assistant principal, I called a parent whose son was being suspended. As I talked with the father and told him what his son had done to be suspended, the father called me a *very* disrespectful name. I took a big breath, counted to seven and replied, "Well, Sir, I understand how you feel, but he *is* suspended. You need to pick him up, and we will see him back on…" (day of week and date).

Now, I had a decision to make. Was it about the father's insult? Was it about me and my innate desire to defend my honor or defend my ethnic origin, or was it about the issue at hand? I decided *not* to allow myself to feel inferior, defensive, furious, vindictive, indignant, righteous, and the list could go on. I was

Wisdom Is the *Principal* Thing!

respectful and said, "Sir." I kept my voice even-toned. I stayed focused on the issue. I *did* my job instead of placing my job in jeopardy. The parent picked his son up that day. I was not in the office at the time, but the secretaries said he did not ask for me or say anything. His son returned to school on the designated date.

I personally feel deep inside that the father knew he was wrong and had crossed the line. Hopefully, he thought about how his tendency to cross the line may have taught a behavior to his son that possibly caused his son to be suspended in the first place. I just remember not having any more problems with that student for the rest of the school year.

Parents may call you names and make untrue accusations. Incidents such as these will enlighten you, so you will know whether or not you are meant to do this job. On the other hand, there will be wonderful, supportive, and caring parents, who will appreciate you and demonstrate it in many awesome ways. This will encourage you. Remember these parents when you feel a bit down-hearted because of something negative a parent has said or done. This remembrance will strengthen you and help you to go on and do what needs to be done for the benefit of all children. Keep the elements of effective conferencing in mind for a great outcome.

Conferences with Parents

PREPARATION

Use Your Journalists' Questions!

1. **Who** needs to be involved in the conference?
   - Administrator
   - Another staff member (psychologist, social worker, staff member for special needs students
   - Counselor
   - District level personnel
   - Parent
   - Teacher
   - Witness (student and/or adult)

2. **What** will be the content of the conference?
   - Academics
   - Discipline
   - Extra-Curricular activities
   - Recognition
   - Special needs

   What type of conference will be held?
   - Email
   - Face-to-face
   - School website portal
   - Telephone
   - Texts (business cellular number)

Wisdom Is the *Principal* Thing!

3. **When** will the conference be held?
    - ➢ Date
    - ➢ Time

4. **Where** will the conference be held?
    - ➢ District level location
    - ➢ Home visitation
    - ➢ School location

5. **Why** do you need *these* people involved? Tell the parent why you have each person present.
    - ➢ It falls within the area of responsibility.
    - ➢ They saw this student's performance or behavior.
    - ➢ The person was requested.

6. **How** will you contact all parties to be involved?
    - ➢ Call
    - ➢ Email or school website portal
    - ➢ Face-to-face
    - ➢ Letter

   How will you conduct the conference?
    - ➢ All involved meet at the same time
    - ➢ Parent first, then call the student into the conference

Conferences with Parents

> ➤ Staff member first, then call the parent and student into the conference

IMPLEMENTATION

It's sad, but in your position, most of your parent conferences will occur because there is a complaint or a need. Very few, if any, parents will set up a conference with you to tell you how great the school is and how happy they are about what the school is doing for their children. Now that you are prepared by answering your journalists' questions, here is what you should do to have effective parent conferences.

1. Be prepared with the information about the issue in front of you. Make certain the referring teacher used the journalists' questions to be thorough and accurate. In other words, do your homework!
2. If you are blind-sided and unaware of a situation, don't make any promises ahead of time because you may end up making a promise that you can't keep. Say you will get more information about it and will get back to him or her, as soon as possible, and *do it*.

Wisdom Is the *Principal* Thing!

3. Use titles and last names, *not* first names (Use Mr., Mrs., Ms., Dr., Reverend, Officer, Sergeant and Professor)
4. Use "Sir" and "Ma'am." This is not being subservient. This says you are showing respect, and you don't think you are better than they are (arrogant) just because you are an administrator.
5. Identify yourself, your area of responsibility ("I'm Ms. Hall and I'm in charge of the 7th graders."). Thank them for agreeing or asking to meet or speak with you, and state the purpose of your conference or call.
6. Have the child in your office to be a part of the face-to-face or telephone conference, if possible. It deters miscommunication.
7. Keep the focus on the issue, not the child. Do not allow yourself to be placed on the defense. Refocus the conversation back to the issue and how the negative behavior is impacting things such as safety, learning, and school operations.
8. Keep your voice *even-toned*, no matter *what* they say.
9. Maintain eye contact when you are in a face-to-face conference, or you will seem like you are hiding something. Don't fiddle, shift, and move papers around your desk more than necessary because it will make you seem shifty or unin-

Conferences with Parents

terested. Remember, this child is one of the most important people on the earth to that parent, so you don't need to appear to minimize the importance of the child or the situation by being quite busy.

10. Let the parent know that you are there to help, not to blame.

11. Describe the offense or need completely but succinctly, using your journalists' questions, of course.

12. Don't say you don't have a choice because you *do*. Don't blame it on the state, the district, and, definitely, not your supervisor. You are, as the administrator, making this choice because the school cannot operate efficiently when what the child has done or has not done negatively impacts school learning, operations, or safety.

13. Be kind, be gentle, and be understanding of how challenging certain news can be to a parent that has a lot going on. Show compassion but not to the point of showing favoritism, acting too quickly, or making unwise decisions.

14. Answer their questions honestly. If you lie or embellish, they will not trust you, and the word will get to the community. If you don't know, say you don't know, but say you *will* find out and get to the bottom of it.

Wisdom Is the *Principal* Thing!

15. Stick to the issue, even when they try to push your buttons out of frustration, anger and disappointment. Keep candy (peppermint, butterscotch, caramel, etc.) in your office. When you offer something, it tells the parent, "I see you as a human being, not just a parental unit!" Many times, it will help break the tension. Refocus unnecessary distractions back to the issue at hand.
16. Keep tissue handy because some parents will cry, and some students will cry. Who knows, *you* might cry!
17. Find *something* complimentary to say about the student (bright, has great potential, is helpful, was honest with you, had good intentions, was very respectful to you, which reflects his great upbringing and so on).
18. Tell the consequence of the infraction, if applicable: Tell exactly how many times, how many days, and the length of times. Tell the positives of an addressed need and the negatives of an unaddressed need. You are right! Just think of your *journalists' questions*! Tell who, what, when, where, why and how the consequence will be administered.
19. Always end with a good action plan. The plan should include expectations for the student, par-

Conferences with Parents

ent, teacher, and administrator. It should have rewards and consequences as well as deadlines and benchmarks.

20. Allow input from all of the participants. Yes, the student too!
21. End on a good note. For example, say, "I hope this will help him to learn how to alert a teacher, rather than trying to address it himself," "This will help him to remember why he is here, so he can be more successful in the classroom," or "I hope this will help to give her the support she needs to improve her grades/behavior." Tell what positive behaviors can potentially result from this experience. A positive attitude helps to build relationships with parents.

FOLLOW-THROUGH

1. Summarize the conference in a letter, a memo, or an email, with receipt options, to the participants and any other pertinent personnel.
2. Make sure all impacted participants and non-participants in the conference know the expected positive outcome. In other words, what will hopefully change and get better?
3. Make sure impacted staff members who were *not* in the conference know the plan.

Wisdom Is the *Principal* Thing!

4. Implement the action plan.
5. Check to see if benchmarks have been met.
6. Update all conference participants, so all can decide if there needs to be an adjustment to the plan or if things are going as everyone had hoped.
7. Adjust the plan or continue as originally intended!

There are many reasons why you may need to have a parent conference. It can be discipline based, curriculum based, special-needs based, or award or recognition based. Positive calls to parents to say something good about a child will show that you value positive things. It will brighten your day too! Whatever the reason for the contact, be wise about deciding whether to have a face-to-face conference or whether a phone call or email will suffice. It takes time, but some things, especially sensitive information pieces, need to be addressed or resolved face-to-face. If you are supporting a teacher who has already had a conference with a parent who is unhappy about her child being placed in a program for children with learning disabilities, and who wants to take the matter higher (which involves you), then you need to have that conference face to face.

Conferences with Parents

They will forget what you said, but they will never forget how you made them feel.

Carl Buehner

CHAPTER 6

CONFERENCES WITH STAFF MEMBERS

Conferences with staff members will have one of two outcomes: positive such as congratulating a teacher for being named the teacher of the year or negative such as disciplining a teacher for an unwise action. You will, most likely, have both types of outcomes during your administrative career.

I have had many conferences with staff members through the years; however, what ensured effectiveness for me were preparation, implementation, and follow-through.

PREPARATION

Use Your Journalists' Questions!

1. **Who** needs to be involved in the conference?
   - Another administrator
   - Curriculum specialist
   - Human Resources personnel
   - Non-certified staff member
   - Teacher, counselor, and another certified staff member

Wisdom Is the *Principal* Thing!

2. **What** will be the content of the conference?
    - Discussion of classroom performance
    - Discussion of extra-curricular involvement
    - Discussion of complaints or requests by parents or students
    - Discussion of requests from a staff member
    - Discussion of requests from the administration

3. **When** will the conference be held?
    - Date
    - Time

4. **Where** will the conference be held?
    - A classroom
    - A conference room
    - A district level office
    - Your office or another office

5. **Why** do you need to have this conference?
    - Administrator request
    - Disciplinary action
    - Evaluation
    - Parent request
    - Student request

Conferences with Staff Members

- Teacher request

6. **How** will you structure this conference?
   - Highlight the *effective* parts of the performance.
   - Note the *ineffective* parts of the performance (things that need to improve).
   - Show *documentation* of effective activities and activities that need improvement.
   - Devise a *plan*

IMPLEMENTATION

1. Have your documentation ready to present in the conference, whether it is in the form of formal observations, informal observations, five-minute walk-throughs, other staff members' concerns, parent emails or letters, or student notes or comments. School districts have forms that you can use for some of your documentation.
2. Take brief notes during the conference. This documentation will help you to compose the summary letter or email.
3. Let the staff member know that your purpose is to be supportive in what he or she is required to do.

Wisdom Is the *Principal* Thing!

4. Let the staff member know the effective things he or she does that positively impact the school. Find *something*! Here are some suggestions:
    - "The kids love you."
    - "The parents love you."
    - "You are always concerned about the safety and well-being of every student."
    - "You get along very well with other teachers."
    - "You are very organized."
    - "You are so willing to help other teachers."
    - "You are willing to help members of the administration, whenever asked."
    - "You have a passion for education. I can see that."
    - "You have gone above and beyond our expectations in that area."
    - "You have been very helpful with extra-curricular activities."
    - "You are always on time for your duty stations."
    - "Your room is so inviting!"
    - "You really help boost morale when you bake those cookies for the staff!"

Conferences with Staff Members

> ➢ "We can always count on you to help with special events."

5. Let the staff member know, *tactfully*, what needs to improve and why it needs to improve. Note these suggestions:
    > ➢ It impacts particular students.
    > ➢ It impacts all of the students.
    > ➢ It hinders learning.
    > ➢ It hinders school operations.
    > ➢ It increases discipline issues.
    > ➢ It causes dissention among staff members.
    > ➢ It diminishes the image of the school.
    > ➢ It leaves students unattended.
    > ➢ It lowers the self-esteem of students.
    > ➢ It lowers the morale of staff members.

6. Help the staff member with a plan for improvement. Allow an opportunity for him or her to give input, and remember the challenges when *you* were in the classroom.

FOLLOW-THROUGH

It is important for the staff member to know that there will be a follow-up to a conference. The following will help:

Wisdom Is the *Principal* Thing!

1. Let the staff member know what you can and are willing to do to support him or her with the improvement goals. For example, say you will do the following:
   - ➢ Provide additional materials and resources
   - ➢ Provide opportunities for support by offering to set up the following:
     - Observing another staff member who is strong in the area that needs improvement
     - Planning with another staff member who is strong in the area that needs improvement
     - Working with the school specialist or a district specialist in the area that needs improvement.
2. Let the staff member know how and how *often* you will check the status of the plan.
3. Let the staff member know when you will have another meeting to discuss the progress.
4. Let the staff member know what actions will follow each conference, pending outcome.
   - ➢ Another observation, partial or full
   - ➢ A five-minute walk-through
   - ➢ A conference with students
   - ➢ A conference with parents

Conferences with Staff Members

> ➢ A conference with other staff members

5. Type the main points of the discussion and the expectations for all parties involved. Make sure everyone receives a copy by memo, letter or email!

Remember, conferences are only as effective as your preparation for them, your communication and your implementation during them, and your follow-through after them. Have all necessary parties involved in the conference and the planning of the next step. Use the journalists' questions to help plan the next step also!

Seek first to understand, and then to be understood.

Stephen R. Covey

CHAPTER 7

CONTACTS

Over time, you may forget who was handy to contact and for what. When you are in a hurry, you should be able to put your hands on what you need. You will not have time for a lot of searching, calling around, and trying to remember, "Just what was that guy's name?" Once you supervise or coordinate a project or program, place every single contact with whom you communicated in that program or project's file for future reference.

PREPARATION

Use Your Journalists' Questions!

1. **Who** supervises that department, program or particular area of responsibility?
2. **What** are their titles?
   What are their responsibilities?
3. **When** are they available?
4. **Where** are they located?
5. **Why** do *you* need them?
6. **How** can you contact them?
   - ➢ Courier information

Wisdom Is the *Principal* Thing!

- Department address
- Email
- Phone number

How can they best help *you* to do *your* job?

IMPLEMENTATION

1. The following are organizations or departments which you may need to contact:
    - Superintendent's office
    - Community organizations
        - Housing Authorities
        - Communities in Schools
        - Home Owners' Associations
    - City, county and school board officials
    - State departments
    - National educational organizations and federal educational departments
    - District departments
        - Attendance—truancy reduction and dropout prevention for students
        - Attendance and retention for the teachers
        - Business, Careers/Vocational
        - Communications

Contacts

- Curricular
    - ✓ Apologetics, Biblical Studies
    - ✓ Curriculum specialists - math and literacy facilitators
    - ✓ English Language Learners
    - ✓ Exceptional Children
    - ✓ Extended academic programs
    - ✓ Fine arts - visual, performing
    - ✓ Foreign Language
    - ✓ Graphics
    - ✓ Life skills
    - ✓ Mathematics
    - ✓ Music (chorus, orchestra and band)
    - ✓ Physical Education/Health
    - ✓ Reading/Language Arts/English
    - ✓ Science/Social Studies
- Discipline
- Extra-Curricular
    - ✓ Academic competitions, clubs, and fairs
    - ✓ Athletics
    - ✓ Intramurals
    - ✓ Speech and debate
- Facilities (maintenance/custodial)

Wisdom Is the *Principal* Thing!

- Food and nutrition
- Licensure and certification
- Mechanics
- Media
  - ✓ Newspapers – major, local and community
  - ✓ Radio
  - ✓ Social Media/Internet
  - ✓ Television
- Media Center equipment, audio visuals, and materials
- Parent groups
- Professional development for staff members
- Police departments
- School security and safety
- Specialty area staff such as nurses, psychologists, social workers, and counselors
- Technology/Computers
- Testing and other assessments
- Transportation

2. The following are typical responsibilities for which you will need to record contact information:

Contacts

- After school activities such as dances and clubs
- Assemblies/Graduations (Contact information will depend on the type of gathering.)
- Athletics
- Cafeteria staff
- Core curriculum specialists
- Custodial staff
- Discipline
- Elective curriculum specialists
- Exceptional and English Language Learners
- Extended-Day programs (After School, Saturday School, Summer School)
- Facilities (maintenance, custodial)
- Fundraising
- Health
- Human Resources (hiring and firing)
- Inventory (furniture, equipment, etc.)
- Itinerant and specialty staff members such as nurses, psychologists, social workers and counselors
- Media Center: books/audio visuals
- Observation and evaluation of staff members

Wisdom Is the *Principal* Thing!

- Parent/Teacher organizations
- Security and safety
- Substitutes
- Technology coordination
- Testing
- Textbooks/curricular materials
- Transportation (bus riders, and parent drop-offs and pick-ups)
- Volunteers

3. You will need detailed information for your list of contacts. Keep this information for every file, hard copy or electronic. Of course, you will already have information for staff members at your school; however, all contact information for parents, district, state, and community personnel should include the following:
   - Name
   - Title/Position
   - Telephone numbers (work and cell, if possible)
   - Email address/website
   - Secretary or assistant's name
   - Hours of operation (Timing!)

Contacts

> ➢ Emergency or alternate personnel's name and number, especially if it is *after normal hours* of operation

This will be very helpful when you need to oversee a project or coordinate a program again. Then, you will have all of the information on that project or program handy with the contact information, and all you will have to do is update.

FOLLOW-THROUGH

Take the time to make notes about how efficiently your contacts operate. I dealt with on-the-ball people. I just did not have the time for excuses. Once I found the most efficient person in that program or department who could help me get the job done, I would communicate with *that* person. If I called, and he or she was not available at the moment, I would leave a voice mail message or send an email because efficient people will return calls and reply to emails promptly. When deciding if persons will be noted as helpful people to contact, ask yourself the following questions:

1. Are they prompt when returning their calls, responding to emails, and getting things done in a timely manner?

Wisdom Is the *Principal* Thing!

2. Are they careful to meet deadlines?
3. Do they care enough to be helpful in aiding *you* to meet *your* deadlines, or do they make excuses?
4. Do they each have a great memory? You will not have time to deal with forgetfulness!
5. Are they trustworthy? Will they do what they *say* they will do?
6. Do they seem to like and respect you? Will they sometimes go above and beyond to be helpful, or do they seem to always be too busy to really give you what you need?

Stay knowledgeable of how the people in certain positions operate, which will allow you to know how to communicate with these particular persons in the future. Build a great network of contacts who are efficient and will communicate effectively with you to help you to accomplish your goals.

You have got to have something in which to believe. You have got to have leaders, organization, friendships, and contacts that help you to believe that, and help you to put out your best.

Dwight D. Eisenhower

CHAPTER 8

CURRICULUM

When I first began interviewing for a principal's position, I was asked how I would approach curriculum at my school. Since I had been heavily involved in the main elements of curriculum at the assistant's level, I was able to discuss with ease how to plan the major components of curriculum. When all is said and done, achievement in the form of test scores, promotions and retentions, grade-level readiness, and the need for extended day programs will play a major part in the decisions that are made about the effectiveness of your school. Curriculum is a vast subject, and the delivery of it was redefined during the 2020 Coronavirus/Covid-19 Pandemic; however, whether teaching online or teaching face to face, you should begin planning with these pertinent components.

PREPARATION

Use Your Journalists' Questions!

1. **Who** needs to learn the content/concept?
    - ➢ Students by grade levels

Wisdom Is the *Principal* Thing!

- Students by subject areas
- Students with special needs
- Students who are English Language Learners (ELL)
- Students who are in advanced or gifted classes
- Students who are impacted by the Professional Learning Communities (PLL)
- Students who are homebound

2. **What** is the content or concept that needs to be learned?
    - Concepts within subject areas
    - Skills that will benefit in all subject areas such as test-taking skills
    - Subject areas

3. **When** do the students need to learn it?
   When do the teachers need to teach it?
    - Before the next concept is taught
    - By district/state standards, timelines, and pacing guides
    - By the end of the quarter
    - By the end of the semester/session
    - By the end of the year
    - During an after-school program
    - During lunch time

Curriculum

- ➢ During a Saturday School Program
- ➢ During a Summer School Program

4. **Where** do the students need to learn it?
   Where will the teachers need to teach it?
   - ➢ In a classroom or laboratory
   - ➢ In the gymnasium
   - ➢ In the Media Center
   - ➢ In the Multi-purpose Room
   - ➢ On a field trip
   - ➢ Online
   - ➢ On the school grounds

5. **Why** does the content or concept need to be learned?
   - ➢ Grade level readiness
   - ➢ Pre-requisite to the next concept
   - ➢ Testing requirement
     - School or district
     - State

6. **How** will the students learn it?
   How will the teachers teach it?
   - ➢ Application
   - ➢ Discovery/Inquiry/Research
   - ➢ Hands-on and problem solving
   - ➢ Hierarchy models
   - ➢ Memorization versus Coding

Wisdom Is the *Principal* Thing!

- Personalized learning (interests)
- Project-Based learning (topics)
- Skill-based Learning (ability and experiences)
- Teacher Appraisal Instrument Models
- Technological Apps or programs

IMPLEMENTATION

1. Learn and apply the Five Important Elements of Curriculum. They will positively or negatively impact your school's effectiveness *very* quickly. Plan with all of these elements in mind:
    - Your School's Data (Math teachers can help you to disaggregate data.)
    - Your Teachers' Classroom Instruction Techniques aligned with state guidelines and standards
    - Your Master Schedule (Chapter 14)
    - Your School Improvement Goals
    - Your School's Curriculum Enhancement Programs for students
        - Academic competitions (tournaments, fairs, bowls, debates)
        - Extended Day programs
        - Tutoring and high interest programs and clubs

Curriculum

2. Learn and apply other factors that can impact your curriculum, immediately or even eventually, dependent upon how you use them. You need to take them into consideration when you plan.
   - Achievement/Readiness levels
   - Availability of funds
     - District
     - Private or business
     - School
     - State
   - Availability of curricular resources
     - Media
     - Written
   - Availability of technology
     - Devices
       - Cell Phones
       - Chromebooks
       - Clickers
       - Computers
         - Desktops
         - Laptops
       - ConnectED, iPad, Mac, TV integration into various curricula, and Apple
       - Tablets

Wisdom Is the *Principal* Thing!

- Programs and software
  - ✓ Applications (Apps)
  - ✓ Discussion boards – Blackboard, Moodle, and Canvas
  - ✓ Discussion Blogs
  - ✓ Electronic portfolios
  - ✓ Google Classroom
  - ✓ Google Docs
  - ✓ Kahoot
  - ✓ Online streaming
  - ✓ Padlet
  - ✓ Podcasts
  - ✓ Thunkable
  - ✓ Virtual fieldtrips
  - ✓ Webinars
  - ✓ Web pages
  - ✓ Zoom/Other meeting Apps
  - ✓ *And so much more!*
- ➢ Availability of school Curriculum Specialists
  - Gifted Learning Specialists
  - Learning Disability Specialists
  - Literacy Specialists
  - Math Specialists
  - Other Curriculum Specialists
- ➢ Availability of district Curriculum Specialists

Curriculum

- Literacy Specialists
- Math Specialists
- Writing Specialists
- Technical Education Specialists
- Testing Specialists
➢ Choice of curriculum
  - District adopted
  - School chosen
  - State adopted
➢ Extended Day programs
  - After school classes
  - After school remediation or enhancement
  - Saturday classes
  - Summer school
➢ Grade levels, departments, and teams
➢ National, state, and district guidelines
➢ Scheduling specifics
  - Daily or A/B classes or alternate in person and virtual learning
  - Length of class periods
  - Length of school day
  - Length of yearly terms (quarters, semesters, sessions, year-round)
  - Student groupings
    ✓ English Language Learning

Wisdom Is the *Principal* Thing!

- ✓ Inclusion
- ✓ Level/Skill
- ➢ School-wide curricular groups
  - Book/Subject area clubs
  - National Honor Society
- ➢ School-wide extra-curricular groups
  - Bands, choirs, and orchestras
  - Chess/other special interest groups
  - Student Councils
- ➢ Special needs
  - Giftedness/Learning Disabilities
  - Autism/Attention Deficit
  - Behavioral/Emotional needs
- ➢ Teacher allotments
- ➢ Teacher licensures/certifications
- ➢ Teacher experience levels
- ➢ Teacher/Pupil ratios

3. Require effective classroom instruction. There are three basic principles of effective instruction:
   - ➢ Determine basic information. *Organize it.*
   - ➢ Present basic information in simplified language with unambiguous examples.
   - ➢ Model the information or process.

4. Require effective classroom techniques.
   - ➢ Being *prepared* to teach, having the information organized and scaffolding

Curriculum

- Getting the students' attention by using an anticipatory set to manage it
- Providing input by introducing concepts to be learned in creative ways
- Modeling by giving examples and by demonstrating examples. Allowing the students also to demonstrate examples, keeping cultural differences in mind.
- Including character education in the teaching techniques
- Enhancing critical thinking skills
- Using technology and using software to enhance student learning. *Critical*!
- Taking the classroom temperature by checking *all* for their understanding and growth (Are they paying attention and on task? Do they understand? Are *my* expectations high enough?)
- Allowing time for all students to interact with the concept through guided practices and activities (This will not only give the teachers needed information about the levels of the students' understanding, but it will also keep the students engaged.)
- Summarizing the concept that was taught to continue observing student

Wisdom Is the *Principal* Thing!

reactions (The teacher *or* the students can summarize.)

➢ Giving independent practices with a task to be completed after class or at home, which will reinforce what was just learned and will give further information to the teacher

➢ Discouraging the tendency of some teachers to require and rely upon rote memorization for learning and testing, while reminding them students must learn to think critically and must interact with information in different ways. After all, students can now use many online search engines to find out anything they need to know. Educators must wake up! The need for walking encyclopedias is *over*!

FOLLOW-THROUGH

1. Learn to be flexible.

    I remember a principal whose school was noted and applauded for significantly raising the students' test scores that particular year. She spoke at a principals' meeting and told us not to be afraid to be creative when placing students.

Curriculum

I agree that for us to ensure students do progress in learning, we must put aside our fears and be flexible when it comes to making sure students are in the most advantageous places for learning. Too many administrators are afraid of labeling or are afraid order will turn into chaos.

2. Move your students around, as needed.
Continually, look at your assessment tools and data, and don't be afraid to move students, accordingly. The principal who was speaking to our group said she was always moving students around. That stuck with me. From your current data information and with teacher input (because there are ways to assess other than by formal testing), consider specific skills that need to be targeted and address them, even if it means you have to move students or teachers. The following are strategies I used and ways you can help your teachers to address weaknesses:

➢ Take a teacher who is strong at teaching a specific skill and switch the teacher with another one, so particular students who are weak in that skill or concept can work with a strong teacher for a couple of days. You do this as needed.

Wisdom Is the *Principal* Thing!

> ➢ Have teachers to demonstrate to the other teachers a specific, creative and exciting way to teach a concept to students.
> ➢ Have teachers to sit in a classroom to observe how another teacher is teaching a particular concept to his or her students.
> ➢ Have strong teachers and not so strong teachers to plan together. I helped arrange for class coverage, when needed.
> ➢ If online learning is applicable, as it was during the 2020 Covid-19 Pandemic, encourage your teachers to share applications (Apps), programs, techniques, and strategies with one another.

No one has all of the answers, and you have to find the answers for *your school's academic success* and *take the risks*. Creativity does *not* have to be chaotic. Just consider all of the elements of curriculum, plan strategically, notify all parties involved, in a timely manner, and implement the plan.

The function of education is to teach one to think intensively and to think critically. Intelligence plus character – that is the goal of true education.

Martin Luther King, Jr.

CHAPTER 9

DIET

Believe it or not, ladies and gentlemen, your diet can impact your performance as an administrator. The decisions you make about your nutrition will have impactful repercussions, short-range and long-range. I was promoted to be an assistant principal after being a teacher in the classroom for 15 years. Being a teacher regulated my eating because I had a lunch period and planning time. Whether I ate in the cafeteria, brought lunch from home, or ate off campus on teacher work days, my position delegated when and where I would eat as well as how much time I had to consume it.

Years later, after 11 years of being a school administrator, I fell and broke my arm. Instead of the typical six weeks to heal, my arm took ten weeks to heal. My doctor thought it was time for me to begin having bone density exams. My first exam results showed I had Osteopenia and was 2 points away from the Osteoporosis range. I was shocked! I thought, "**What? I am 48 years old, not 80! How could this be?**" After much reflection, I did contribute it to 11 years of running around a school, either not eating at all or not eating healthily. Guess what I

Wisdom Is the *Principal* Thing!

would do to keep going? You guessed it: Drink coffee! I would grab a cup of coffee in the morning to substitute for breakfast, and then I would drink five to six cups of coffee a day to get that caffeine kick and keep moving. If there was an afternoon or evening school event I had to supervise, guess what? Yes! I would drink even more coffee. Sometimes, I would grab a candy bar or pack of cheese crackers and a soda on the way to supervise an after-school event. My body simply did not get enough calcium, so I lost bone mass.

As a new administrator, you will experience different eating tendencies because you have so much to do, and you have school level responsibilities you haven't had before. Many either don't eat, or they eat, but they eat on the run and unhealthily. Many cram snacks into their mouths when they find a moment. All of these are not healthy and can cause a variety of health problems, sooner or later!

So, please, be wise. Plan your eating. Schedule your meals as much as possible in advance. Keep up with the research on foods. You may be allergic to something and not know it! "Oh, that's why I'm keeping this post-nasal drip!" Get your physical, once a year! I hate to think what would have happened to me if I had not broken my arm, and if my doctor had not ordered a bone density exam. Pay

Diet

attention to your own body. I was having terrible backaches and did not know that it was because I had lost bone mass in my spine over the years.

PREPARATION

Use Your Journalists' Questions!

1. **Who** will you allow to impact your eating habits?
    - Who will bring you food?
    - Who will eat with you?
    - Who will take you out to eat?
    - Who will be responsible for preparing your food?
        - You
        - Your co-workers
        - Your district colleagues
        - Your friends
        - Your principal
        - Your secretary
        - Your family members

2. **What** will you eat?
    - Food from the school cafeteria
    - Food brought from home

Wisdom Is the *Principal* Thing!

- Food parents and students bring for you
- Junk food
- Nutritious food
- Pre-paid and pre-prepared meals

3. **When** will you eat?
    - Any time of the day
    - Between the end of the school day and after school events
    - Between school activities
    - Breakfast time
    - Dinner time
    - Lunch time

4. **Where** will you eat?
    - Faculty and academic meetings
    - Nearby fast food places
    - Nearby restaurants
    - School cafeteria
    - Teachers' Lounge or classroom
    - Workshops/Conferences
    - Your office or another's office

5. **Why** will you eat?
    - It is expected, and you need to appear sociable.

Diet

- ➤ It is time.
- ➤ You are hungry.
- ➤ You are stressed and need a snack.
- ➤ Your diet controls health conditions.

6. **How** will you eat? How much will you eat?
    - ➤ Eat just a bite or a snack, enough to keep moving.
    - ➤ Eat on the run.
    - ➤ Eat until full.
    - ➤ Eat, taking your time.

IMPLEMENTATION

If you do not schedule times to eat, just like anything else, eating will become habitual all by itself. Be methodical about eating, just as you are about the other things you must do.

1. Schedule times to eat.
2. Eat one meal and at least one healthy snack during the day
3. Bring your lunch and snack from home, during student days. You will eat much healthier than if you try to grab something from the cafeteria or elsewhere.

Wisdom Is the *Principal* Thing!

4. Plan and suggest to your colleagues a few healthy places to eat on teacher work days.
5. Get regular checkups with the doctor to make sure you are receiving the amount of nutrition you should.

FOLLOW-THROUGH

Now that you have great plans to eat much healthier, when the best laid plans of mice and men go astray, and they will, try to *balance* the kinds of food you eat.

1. When you are attending a workshop or a meeting where food is provided, limit the eating of the unhealthy foods. You do *not* have to pile your plate high or *keep* going back.
2. When food is flowing, eat more of the veggies, fruits and grilled or baked foods.
3. When students and parents bring you cookies, candies, and other high calorie foods, eat one in their presence to make them feel appreciated, thank them, and then tell them you are saving some for later to do one of the following:
    ➤ To share with other office staff members

Diet

- ➢ To share and offer to non-certified staff, who are often underappreciated
- ➢ To share with spouse or kids at home
- ➢ To save some to eat tomorrow.
4. If checkups with the doctor reveal abnormal nutritional levels, ask for recommendations for adjusting your eating habits.
5. Follow your doctor's instructions!

I strongly encourage you to eat. You will need your strength to do this job. However, I encourage you to develop a nutrition plan for yourself; otherwise, your eating habits will develop themselves, dependent upon your schedule and energy levels. If you do not discipline yourself with eating, your habits will be driven by hunger, availability, frustration, and stress. Eventually, this will impact your performance in one way or another. You are what you eat, right? So, be wise, and eat healthily!

The first and greatest victory is to conquer yourself.

Plato

CHAPTER 10

DISCIPLINE

The teacher is responsible for the discipline *within the classroom*. The administrator is usually responsible for the discipline *at the school level*. Discipline is *addressed differently* by school districts and systems, according to the population of students, number of students, grade levels of schools, facilities, other staff members, and school types such as public, private, traditional, Montessori, charter, or religious (Christian and Islamic).

Just remember, the most important lesson you can get your teachers to learn is this: The more engaged in and excited about learning the students are and the better the relationships between the students and the teachers are, the less discipline concerns the teachers will have. However, when dealing with the disciplining of students, be proactive.

PREPARATION

Use Your Journalists' Questions!

1. **Who** is within my area of responsibility? **Who** is assigned to me for discipline?

Wisdom Is the *Principal* Thing!

- Students by grade levels
- Students by alphabet
- Students by assigned areas - Media Center, gymnasium, auditorium, multi-purpose room, cafeteria at lunch time or other areas such as halls, buildings, floors, or outside during free time

2. **What** are my options concerning discipline?
   What disciplinary measures are allowed for my school?
   - District procedures
   - School procedures
   - State procedures
     - School-wide discipline plan
     - Department discipline plans
     - Individual teacher discipline plans
     - Team discipline plans

3. **When** may I address discipline referrals?
   - After school
   - Before school
   - During class times
   - During lunch times

   When must I have discipline issues resolved?
   - The day of the offense

Discipline

- ➤ The day after the offense
- ➤ 24 – 48 hours
- ➤ When the investigation is completed

4. **Where** may I discipline students?
    - ➤ In my office
    - ➤ In a teacher's classroom
    - ➤ In the area of the offense

    Where may I assign students for the consequence?
    - ➤ Cafeteria
    - ➤ Classroom
    - ➤ Home
    - ➤ Outside

5. **Why** do I need to discipline a particular student or group of students?
    - ➤ They were disobeying classroom rules.
    - ➤ They were disobeying schoolwide rules.
    - ➤ They were disrespecting staff members.

6. **How** may I discipline these students?
    - ➤ Lightly for minor infractions
    - ➤ Severely for serious and dangerous infractions

Wisdom Is the *Principal* Thing!

IMPLEMENTATION

There are similarities that run through all types of schools when it comes to discipline: Types of referrals for misbehavior, ways of addressing referred students, types of discipline, types of documentation, ways to contact parents, and ways to supervise in the classroom and at duty stations. Implement the major elements for improving student behavior.

1. Know the part of the population for which you are responsible: Discipline can be *assigned to school administrators differently*, according to levels. Most assignments for discipline are as follows:
    - Charter and private schools often assign disciplinarians for *all* students, depending on the size of the school.
    - Public elementary schools typically assign a grade level or a group of levels such as primary school grades or upper elementary school grades.
    - Public middle schools typically assign by a grade level.
    - Public high schools typically assign either by a portion of the alphabet or by a grade level.

Discipline

> Public K-8 schools typically assign a grade level or a group of levels such as primary, upper elementary, or middle school.

2. Make sure teachers are accurate and thorough reporters when they refer. Although schools refer discipline incidents differently, documentation will need to be specific. Words like "bad," "disruptive," or "too talkative" and "disrespectful" are *too* general. Parents will ask you, "So, what does that mean?" "What did he specifically say?" or "What did she do that was so disrespectful?"

Once, I received a referral from a teacher which said the student was very "disrespectful." Upon further investigation, I discovered that the student had been respectful when answering the teacher but refused to say, "***Sir.***" Since the teacher had notified the parent about the incident also, I received the longest email from that parent accusing the teachers of requiring kids, especially Black kids, to be subservient. I had a time trying to smooth that situation out! Teach staff members not only to be specific when they refer but to also refrain from making their own past experiences a policy. Cultural differences also must be

Wisdom Is the *Principal* Thing!

taken into consideration. If that referring teacher had been more specific on the referral by clarifying what he considered disrespectful, I would have been able to talk with the teacher, hopefully, before he contacted the parent. Referrals will be more specific and have more clarity when the person who is referring uses the journalists' questions. Here is an example of a specific referral:

> - **Who** did he do it to? *Sally Green*
> - **What** specifically did he do? *He picked up his notebook, walked over to Sally and hit her on the head with the notebook.*
> - **When** did he do it? *He did it right after lunch time, approximately 12:30 p.m.*
> - **Where** did he do it? *He did it in the classroom.*
> - **Why** did he say he did it? *He said he did it because Sally jumped in front of him in the lunch line when they were in the cafeteria.*
> - **How** did it end? *Sally started crying, and I immediately took the notebook and marched him to the office.*

Discipline

Requiring teachers to use the journalists' questions will help to make sure the teachers are specific, which, in turn, will not only help answer parent questions but will also help you as the administrator make an *informed decision* concerning the consequence.

3. Aid teachers with discipline. As an administrator, teachers need you to do the following:
    - Know your federal, state, district, and school policies.
    - Pay attention to the student make up of all classrooms: Do not place concentrations of Special Needs students or students with hefty discipline records in one classroom. I allowed teams, grade levels and departments to submit names to counselors of students who needed to be separated, so they would not be together in one class. Do what you can *feasibly* do.
    - Computers will often schedule classes with concentrated groups of kids who are known for causing problems in the classroom. It's depressing for the teachers and it kills their motivation. Find a way to give some relief. Spread the students with a history of

Wisdom Is the *Principal* Thing!

discipline issues *throughout* the classes. Change schedules, rotate students, and break up clicks that *don't* encourage each other to do the right thing. For my middle school, at registration time, I used to have the counselors to ask the elementary school personnel to alert us about those who were feeding into our school, who did not need to be on the same team and *definitely* not in the same classroom.

➢ Provide workshops and trainings, so teachers can have opportunities to learn new strategies.

➢ Provide opportunities for shadowing. Allow opportunities for new teachers and teachers who are struggling to observe a teacher who is a strong disciplinarian.

➢ Allow team, department or school-wide discipline plans, according to the needs of your school.

➢ Help teachers to develop and to implement classroom discipline plans. Give them information from sample plans that have proven to be effective.

➢ Give basic recommendations for

Discipline

proven classroom discipline plans:
- Plans must clearly state expectations for behavior.
- Plans must state the *consequence* for each offense.
- Plans must also state *rewards* for good behavior.
- Plans must maintain *consistency* and *equity* for *all* students.

➤ Teach teachers the following:
- *How* to be consistent. Consistency is one of the biggest problems for new teachers. Some teachers, especially new ones, have difficulty with giving the same consequence to one student, who is usually great and obedient, and another student, who seems to always do something wrong. They need to have, for the same infraction, the same consequences, no matter *who* the students may be, unless there are extenuating circumstances. Here is an example to think about: If something happened recently to a student that was traumatic such as a divorce or a death in the family, it should be taken into consideration by all, and a

fair decision should be made, concerning how to deal with the behavior; otherwise, give the same consequence.

- How they should *not* take discipline matters *personally*. Some teachers have a difficult time with remembering that children will be children. A teacher cannot feel that the student said something or did something *to him* or *her*. Tell them that students will misbehave sometimes, and it has nothing to do with who the teacher is. It *can* have something to do with the circumstances; for example, the opportunity to throw a spitball because the teacher is not watching can motivate some students, or problems at home may cause a student to act out, as previously noted.

- How to research to find out what really happened, so there is no doubt that the offense deserves the consequence. Some students are not accurate reporters, as we all know. Tell teachers that doing their homework will gain respect from students and

Discipline

parents, and they will gain a reputation for being fair.

- How to effectively get to the root of the problem. There are so many reasons students may misbehave:
  - ✓ Abuse
  - ✓ Attention
  - ✓ Boredom
  - ✓ Different expectations from home to school
  - ✓ Embarrassment/low self-esteem
  - ✓ Excitement
  - ✓ Fear of failure
  - ✓ Hunger
  - ✓ Illness
  - ✓ Medical conditions unaddressed
  - ✓ Negligence
  - ✓ Peer pressure and bullying
  - ✓ Power - They have been previously rewarded for misbehavior, and they liked it.
  - ✓ Revenge
  - ✓ Sleepiness
  - ✓ Special needs unidentified
  - ✓ Stress
  - ✓ Worry about issues at home

Wisdom Is the *Principal* Thing!

- How to discipline students without verbally abusing, stereotyping, name calling, or humiliating them
- How discipline should teach the students the benefits of behaving to encourage the students to *want* to behave. Discipline should enlighten the student. It is not to induce fear. If it induces fear, it is just punishment.
- How to engage the aid of specialty staff members—psychologists, social workers, dropout prevention staff, counselors, and security personnel as well as how to engage volunteers.
- How to effectively communicate with the parents by teaching phrases to teachers emphasizing their responsibility to educate *all* children, while not allowing distractions that prevent teaching and learning.
- How to work with the many supportive parents, while also working with parents who will try to intimidate the teacher because they do not want to deal with the issues that lie within their families.
- How to compliment the students in some way, so their interactions with the students and their parents don't seem to always be negative.

Discipline

- How to develop a *relationship* with all students, which can lead to several positive results such as their behaving for the following reasons:
    - ✓ Because they like the person
    - ✓ Because they respect the person
    - ✓ Because they do not want to disappoint the person
    - ✓ Because they do not want to embarrass the person

    They often will make the teacher aware of home and environmental issues, which may have an impact on their attitudes or behaviors.

4. Address discipline, *promptly*. Deal with it! You probably have heard, "It's a nasty job, but somebody has to do it." Well, unless you are fortunate enough to be hired for curriculum assignments only, that's going to be you. Not addressing discipline issues promptly will lead to bigger problems.

    ➤ Teachers may feel that you are not supporting them and all that they have to do in the classroom.

    ➤ Students in the classroom will think they can get away with things and misbehave

Wisdom Is the *Principal* Thing!

even more. Small problems that require light disciplinary actions will become larger problems, which will, unfortunately, require stronger discipline.
➢ Parents who are contacted three or four days after the incident may express the fact that you did not immediately deal with it and did not let them know in a timely manner. They will say things like this: "That happened three days ago. Why am I just hearing about it now?" or "If you had called me right away when he did the first offense, I would have dealt with it, and he would not have done the second offense."

Strategies that will help you address discipline promptly are as follows:
➢ Schedule times on your calendar to work on discipline, just as you would block out times on your calendar to have conferences. Designate a time. Don't say, "I'll deal with referrals when I have the time." It won't happen. There will *always* be something else that will need your attention.
➢ Rotate times with another assistant principal or key staff member. One assistant

Discipline

principal can cover emergencies while one assistant principal does referrals. Make sure these times do not cause you to be consistently unavailable to the same teachers.

➤ Treat discipline referrals like a conference you must have or a teacher evaluation you must do. Sometimes an emergency may happen, so you may have to stop and deal with it (student trips a fire alarm). If you must leave your office, plant students strategically *i.e.* counselor's office, secretary's office, outer office, or another assistant principal's office. You definitely don't want to come back to an additional problem. If you call a student from the referring teacher's classroom, try not to send the student back to his or her classroom until you have addressed the referral, or it may appear to the teacher and the other students that the referred student got away with the offense.

➤ Have a sign that you can place on your door that says, "In conference, thank you for waiting." This will deter some interruptions when you are having conferences with students.

Wisdom Is the *Principal* Thing!

- Call more than one student to your office at a time. People will respect the fact that you have students in your office. Teachers, counselors, parents, and other administrators will see you are encumbered and, hopefully, not think, "She's not *that* busy." If it is something that can wait, they will wait or go away and come back. If people only see one student in your office, trust me, they will think you are not *that* busy and often will interrupt or wait and expect you to deal with their issues as soon as you finish with that one student. There goes your plan to discipline for the next hour.
- Weigh how many students you should call to your office for a certain period of time, and take the following into consideration:
  - Age and grade level
  - Gender
  - Type of offense
  - Rival groups or gangs
  - Students you may not want to have in your office at the same time.
    Eliminate opportunities for conflicts or shenanigans.
  - Offenses requiring light discipline (lunch time or after school detention)

Discipline

- Offenses requiring moderate discipline (in-school suspension)
- Offenses requiring heavy discipline (out-of-school suspension)
- Offenses requiring severe discipline (exclusion/expulsion)

> Consider students who have gotten into a conflict, not to mention a fight, and decide whether to have them in the office at the same time. Be careful with racial tensions, gender tensions, bullying, economic differences, and neighborhood rivalries. You do not want a knock-down, dragged out fight in your office or in your office area! Then the issue will become you and *your* lack of control, even in the office area! That would not be good.

5. Make *sure* the consequence fits the offense. When you are tired, cranky, hungry, frustrated, overwhelmed or not having a good day, sometimes, there is a tendency for *overkill*. Suppress it! Here are some proven suggestions for assigning negative consequences and rewarding good behavior.

Wisdom Is the *Principal* Thing!

Negative Consequences

- Inactive Detention: Before school and after-school detention, time-out, lunch detention, and recess detention, where students sit quietly and are not allowed to participate with the other students' and in the usual activities.
- Active detention: Lunch or recess, where they are assigned to staff (Sometimes cafeteria staff members will help and have them to clean tables and sweep the floor.) Before and after school, where they are assigned to custodians to pick up paper on school grounds or assigned to a teacher to do chores. Have gloves for them, and if you choose after school detention, verify transportation home first.
- Restriction from fun activities
- In-school suspension: This takes additional staff. Students are assigned to a designated room, and teachers send assignments to the room for the student to complete.
- Out-of-school suspension: Students are suspended out of school for the rest of a day or for a number of days, depending on the offense. If transportation is a complicated

Discipline

> issue, the student can be sent to in-school suspension for the rest of the day or can be transported home by a staff member, with the parent's permission. Consider alternatives for *elementary* school kids.
>
> ➤ Exclusion/Expulsion: Serious offenses that involved a weapon, drugs, theft, or fighting that caused serious injuries. Students may not attend their assigned schools. They are either assigned to a special school for excluded students, or they are not allowed to attend any school in that district for a specific amount of time.

Positive Consequences

> ➤ Announcements in the classroom, on the school intercom, in the school newsletter, or on the school website
> ➤ Assemblies
> ➤ Assisting the teacher
> ➤ Caring for the classroom pet
> ➤ Free time – game time, computer time
> ➤ Field trips and special visitations
> ➤ Media Center time. Have an agreement with the media specialist.
> ➤ Note or call to the students

Wisdom Is the *Principal* Thing!

- ➤ Note to go help another staff member: Have an agreement with that staff member first.
- ➤ Note or call to the parents
- ➤ Stickers, trinkets, and treasure boxes
  Be creative!

6. Document how you are addressing discipline.
   - ➤ Use your *Daily Log* (Chapter 12) for documentation. Noting the basics on your log will be a quick reference for you. Put the date, time, student name, type of contact, concern or result (offense and resolution). Your log, whether electronic or hard copy, will also be helpful if you need documentation for something such as a contact log for a critical conference or exclusion hearing.
   - ➤ Use incident reports. Have the students to complete an incident report to tell their side of the story. Whether a student was a victim, perpetrator or witness, this will accomplish the following:
     - More often than not, a student will tell what he or she did or did *not* do more accurately when writing what happened the *first* time.

Discipline

- It is proof to parents that you allowed the student to tell his or her side of the story.
- It is documentation, in case the student tries to change his story later, when he finds out how much trouble he is *really* in. Some students are not accurate reporters, especially when they get in front of their parents, not to mention friends (They don't want to be labeled a "snitch.").
- You can find similarities between the written reports and have more chances to find out what *really* happened (who really started the fight). You can get to the bottom of it much more quickly than just listening to several of the students talk and trying to sort it out audibly.
- It is documentation for your files to view and use as needed.
- It gives you some time to make a phone call or do something else while the student is writing (multi-tasking).

➢ Use the journalists' questions on incident reports.

Wisdom Is the *Principal* Thing!

- **Who** was involved in the incident, including your part? **Who** were the witnesses to the incident?
- **What** happened, in your own words?
- **When** did the incident occur?
- **Where** did the incident occur?
- **Why** did the incident occur?
- **How** did the incident end? **How** did the teacher respond?

➤ Have the student to sign the report with the following statement:

This statement is true and made of my own free will and accord.

_____
Student Signature

➤ Add district school forms that are required for documentation. Store them in a folder with the student's name on it.

7. Assign a schedule of duty stations. Duty stations are usually included in the dean, vice or assistant principal's scope of responsibilities. Manned duty stations such as restrooms and other key areas of the school will deter much mischief! I was told by a principal that the previous school year, a boy peeked over the wall of a restroom stall to see another student using the

Discipline

toilet. The spy laughed and called the other student, "Winkie-Dinkie!" A fight ensued like no other that year! No one can be everywhere at once; however, you, as an administrator, can be effective in preventing many problems (including bullying, fighting and playing pranks) by having a plan that assigns duty stations. There is nothing like a serious incident that occurred because no teacher or administrator was around to deter it.

➢ Use mediations to resolve differences.
➢ Be proactive: Plan for anything that could occur.
➢ Be visible: There are critical times when administrators need to be visible.
- After testing times
- Arrival of students to school
- Assembly times
- Dismissal of students from school
- Emergencies
- Exchange of classes
- Extra-Curricular event times
- Field trip times
- Lunch times (before, after, during)
- Recess and other breaks
- Restroom times

Wisdom Is the *Principal* Thing!

- Safety Drills
> Require teachers and other staff members to be visible in their assigned areas during these same times unless they are already assigned to a group of students.
> Require other staff members, especially those working directly with students, such as counselors and security personnel, to be visible in all places where students gather during non-class times. Some places where students congregate and potential problems may be deterred are as follows:
  - Athletic fields and dugouts
  - Behind or beside buildings
  - Bleacher areas
  - Bus lots
  - Cafeterias
  - Court yards
  - Flag poles
  - Hallways (Teachers can also stand in front of their classroom doors at key times.)
  - Malls
  - Nooks, crannies and corners
  - Patios
  - Playgrounds and other play areas

Discipline

- Quad areas
- Restrooms
- Stairwells

Give staff members rotation schedules, so they will know expected duty procedures. Note: Even if some staff members volunteer to do duty assignments all of the time, rotate them anyway. Spread the responsibilities of supervising duty stations because those same volunteers will burn out.

FOLLOW-THROUGH

1. Whatever discipline you give, contact a *parent or guardian*. These contacts may take many forms:
    - A face-to-face conference requested by you, the parent, or a staff member
    - A note mailed to the student's home, but require a parent signature and the note to be returned. If the note is not returned, call or email the parent.
    - A note sent home by the student. If you send it, send it for very minor infractions, require a parent signature, and check with the parent if the note is not returned.
    - A telephone call to the parent

Wisdom Is the *Principal* Thing!

> An email to the parent

Be *sure* to note information on your *Daily Log*.

2. Whatever discipline you must give, contact the *teacher or other staff member* involved. Contacts may also take many forms:
    > Face-to-face conferences
    > Notes or memos in the teachers' boxes
    > Emails
    > Copies of referrals with consequences given (*highly recommended*)

3. Whatever discipline you give, provide opportunities for rewards for *improved* behaviors. You can work with the referring staff member to do this. Working with students and seeing their behaviors improve is encouraging to all.

Addressing discipline can be one of the hardest parts of an administrator's job. Although it teaches the children how they should behave, it often draws negativity and can be downright depressing. I would go home at the end of my day and feel like all I did was literally discipline students all day. This is why you must take the times to view the *good things* that are going on in your school. You need to conduct

Discipline

observations anyway, so go to observe a class where something neat is going on, even if you only have time for a five or ten-minute walk-through. Go to a performing arts class and listen to the choir, orchestra, or band. You can even clap when they finish a song. The teacher and the students will love it! Go to the gym or cafeteria and positively interact with students and teachers. It's refreshing to them *and* to you!

These moments will remind you of what it is all about: Educating students so they will grow up to be critical thinkers, productive members of society, and positive, successful contributors in this world. This is the big picture. This is what makes it all worthwhile.

We need to understand the difference between discipline and punishment. Punishment is what you do to someone; discipline is what you do for someone.

Zig Ziglar

CHAPTER 11

EXTENDED DAY PROGRAMS

Most schools have some type of extended day or extended year program to address academic weaknesses. Many are week days, where the days are extended for two to three hours, Saturdays for half a day, or summer programs for several weeks. While they can be challenging, these programs are great opportunities for an aspiring principal to gain experience. It's like running your own mini-school because you have to coordinate all of the components of the program, which are similar to the day programs but smaller and more specialized.

You have to hire the staff, choose the curriculum, develop the master schedule, develop the discipline and safety procedures, and develop the duty station assignments for teachers. You have to coordinate the feeding availabilities, transportation procedures, and effective communications with teachers, students, and parents. *The works*! So, when you are assigned to coordinate an extended day program, don't panic. It's easy if you are organized, and if you implement the main components.

Wisdom Is the *Principal* Thing!

PREPARATION

Use Your Journalists' Questions!

1. **Who** will need to be involved in the program?
   - Administrators
   - Teachers
   - Other staff members
     - Bus Drivers
     - Community tutors and mentors
     - Counselors
     - Custodians
     - Secretaries
     - Security Personnel

2. **What** will be the content (curriculum and other activities) of the program?
   - Alternate learning activities and learning styles
   - Different or new lesson plans
   - Hands-on activities
   - Lab activities
   - Repeated lesson plans
   - Seat work
   - Technology and proven software
   - Testing strategies

Extended Day Programs

3. **When** will the program be in effect?
   When will you need staff and students to be in their places?
   - Dates
   - Times

4. **Where** will the program be located?
   Where do you need everyone to be stationed during the program?
   - Bus Lot
   - Cafeteria
   - Classrooms and laboratories
   - Gymnasium
   - Media Center
   - Multipurpose Room
   - Outside locations
   - School-wide student gathering areas or contained areas for the program

5. **Why** do you need these staff members involved?
   - Availability, interests and requests
   - Knowledge of concepts to be taught
   - Licensure/Certification
   - Special skills in needed areas
   - Staff members interests and requests

   Why do these particular students need to be included in the program?

Wisdom Is the *Principal* Thing!

- ➢ Grades and grade level readiness
- ➢ Parent or student requests
- ➢ Teacher recommendations
- ➢ Test scores

6. **How** will you contact the teachers, the students and the parents?
   How will you contact district departments that are critical for the success of your program?
   - ➢ Courier services
   - ➢ Emails, letters or memos
   - ➢ Face-to-face
   - ➢ Parent portals and school websites
   - ➢ Telephone calls
   - ➢ Zoom or other group applications

IMPLEMENTATION

With the journalists' questions in mind, use these key steps to design and implement an extended day program:

1. Decide the dates, locations and times for the program.
2. Identify the students who should be in the program by these: achievement scores, failure rates, absentee rates, and teacher recommendations.

Extended Day Programs

3. Decide the budget needs and requirements.
4. Choose the curriculum for the program, including pre-testing and post-testing to note progress. Gain guidance and input from the teachers in the program.
5. Set the registration dates and times. Recruit who will be in charge of registration.
6. Recruit teachers and other staff members: administrative assistants, teacher assistants, secretaries, custodians, and counselors for the program. Have announcements, sign-up venues, and confirmations, whether written or technological.
7. Choose your leadership team out of the recruits. Make sure that they have the skills to aid you in developing, implementing, and supervising an effective program. Then, delegate and empower *them*.
8. Set up transportation procedures. Yes! Use your journalists' questions.
    ➢ Procedures for parents dropping the children off and picking them up
    ➢ Make sure your staff member who will supervise the transportation at the school as well as the *district's* transportation officer have the following information for all students attending.

Wisdom Is the *Principal* Thing!

- Names, telephone numbers, and addresses of all students who are riding the bus
- Dates for the beginning and ending of the program
- Arrival and dismissal times for the program
- Contact information for the staff member who is in charge of the transportation

➢ Procedures for the bus riders and drivers

➢ Bus routes and procedures that should be included in the initial letter to the parents. Allow time to adjust plans, if needed.

9. Design the food/nutrition program.
   ➢ Cafeteria involvement
   ➢ Lunch time
   ➢ Snack time
10. Send information to other staff members for awareness, even those who are not involved.
11. Send information to parents by mail or by students. Information can be attached to report cards, sent in email groups, or sent by automated telephone systems. Have an effective back-up plan if letters that are mailed or sent by students

Extended Day Programs

are not returned promptly by having staff members to call the parents. If none of these efforts are successful, call the student and inform the student that he or she will have to repeat the grade unless the letter is signed. The student will most likely make sure the parent signs the letter. An incentive can be given to students who do return letters. All letters to parents should include the following:

- ➢ Food availabilities/opportunities
- ➢ Financial fees/costs, if applicable.
- ➢ Name of the coordinator and the contact for questions
- ➢ Program dates and times
- ➢ Registration dates and times
- ➢ Statement explaining to parents why their students are being assigned to the program. Keep it positive.
- ➢ Transportation procedures, once they are confirmed by the school district transportation department. If transportation procedures are not confirmed, the letter can note that bus routes will be sent in a separate mailing. Don't forget!

12. Set up a mail box system and an email group for extended day staff members. Include the option for online meetings with Zoom or other avenues.

13. Meet with extended day staff members to discuss the operation of the program. Give all of the staff members a folder, which contains this pertinent information:
    - A copy of the master schedule, which should include subject assignments, grade-level assignments, room assignments, and locations for all meetings and activities.
    - A copy of the daily schedule with arrival and departure times, lunch and break times, and class times for both students and teachers
    - A copy of class lists and pertinent information about students such as addresses, telephone numbers and additional parent contact information.
    - A copy of attendance sheets and procedures
    - A copy of discipline procedures and referral forms to be used
    - A copy of the teacher duty roster, including hall duty, bus and parking lot duty, and any other teacher expectations
    - A copy of general procedures
      - Communication

Extended Day Programs

- Emergency procedures
- Fire drills
- Lockdown procedures
- Tornado drills
> A copy of procedures for requesting supplies
> A schedule of staff meetings
> A schedule of pay dates
> A contact sheet that requests their personal information
- Names
- Email addresses
- Licensure and certification information
- Mailing addresses
- Telephone numbers
> A copy of expectations concerning instructional techniques and procedures. Emphasize "No busywork!" Include a copy of a teacher observation form.
> Information on the curriculum to be used and who to contact to receive it
> Information stating who to contact for audio-visuals, technology, keys, and other materials

Wisdom Is the *Principal* Thing!

FOLLOW-THROUGH

It is imperative that you double-check *every* element of the program just as you would for the opening of the regular school year. Before the first day of the program and during the program, make sure the following are in place:

1. Make sure *your* promises are kept. Hold *yourself* accountable first.
2. Guide your leadership team in guiding persons who are under their authority to help all successfully complete their tasks.
3. Get regular feedback from the leadership team concerning the progress with their assigned tasks.
4. Find out if there are barriers to the success of the program, and if so, remove them.
5. Do your own walk-throughs of classrooms and other areas to assess the readiness of the program and to maintain effectiveness.
6. Resist the urge to micro-manage by doing something or re-doing something yourself that is assigned to your team member. Support and work *with* your leadership team.

Extended Day Programs

As with any program, assess the effectiveness and debrief by doing the following, which will help you to supervise an even better program the next time:
1. Make notes of the issues, flaws and successes that occurred during the program.
2. Obtain input from your leadership team about the program's success.
3. Place the debriefing information with your other files on extended day programs.

Please note that childcare programs, which are before and after school are a little different from regular extended day programs because most will have procedures that are required by the district. Whoever is in charge of these childcare programs will receive training and instructions from outside of the school. However, this chapter's information will be helpful for the success of *any* school-level, extended day program.

The best executive is the one who has sense enough to pick good men to do what he wants done, and self-restraint to keep from meddling with them while they do it.

Thaddeus Hammond

CHAPTER 12

FILE ORGANIZATION

Believe it or not, things will come at you so fast that you will not remember who you talked to, when you talked to him or her, what you talked about, what *you* are supposed to do (what *your action step* needs to be) after the contact is over, and finally, how you need to keep track of that information you just received. Things will quickly become complicated or overwhelming if you do not have an efficient system in place for keeping various types of information that you give and receive.

PREPARATION

Let's begin with my quick reference system that would at many times prevent the need to go to a *detailed* hard copy or electronic file. Keep a daily log to quickly check those you contacted by conference, phone or email.

Use Your Journalists' Questions!

1. **Who** sent you the information that needs to be noted, organized, and filed?

2. **What** information needs to be noted, organized, and filed?
3. **When** does the information need to be noted, organized, and filed?
4. **Where** did you receive the information from, and where does it need to be noted, organized, and filed?
5. **Why** did you receive the information, and why do you need to note it, organize it, and file it (awareness or action required)?
6. **How** did you receive the information (letter, memo, email, phone call, or face-to-face conference), and how do you need to respond to it, note it, organize it, and file it?

IMPLEMENTATION

A part of efficient filing is to keep documentation that you can reference and access quickly by logging it. Your co-workers (secretaries, counselors, or other assistants), your parents and students, and your supervisors, principals and district personnel will love the fact that you can quickly look through your *Daily Log* and tell them who you talked to, when you talked to them, and what the outcome was. If more detailed information is needed on the issue, then you can pull the file that includes more documentation.

File Organization

1. Keep a *Daily Log*. Mine resembled this one:

Name	Date	Time	How Rcv'd	Concern	Result
Ms. Blue, Dick's Mom	3/5/17	9:15	F2F	Cursed teacher	3 days OSS & Ms. Blue was supportive.
Reg. Supt.	3/6/17	5:30 pm	Rcv'd Email	Parent complaint. Mr. Tallguy	Gave info. She will call parent and support me!

> Note the journalists' questions for using your log!
> - The name of the person (*Who*?), the *date*, and the *time (When?)* will not only help you to remember but will be proof of your dealing with issues, especially concerning students and parents.
> - The recording of how the contact was received will remind you of whether you *called* a number or received a call from it. This will enable you to have the option of re-calling or returning a call. It also will remind you if it was *a face-to-face* conference or

Wisdom Is the *Principal* Thing!

> an email to which you need to respond (***Where?***).
> - The ***concern*** records the purpose, which is the ***Why***, and records the issue, which is the ***What*** of the call or conference.
> - The ***result*** will record the resolution of the problem or will remind you of ***How*** you still need to proceed as a result of the conference.

➢ Use a simple, spiral notebook or something similar, which is small enough to not take up much space but is large enough to hold your notes. Use either something that slips easily into a handbag or briefcase or something that can be easily retrieved, electronically. You can create a template of this on your computer, tablet or cell phone. Do *whatever* works best for *you*! This documentation could be used for letters, emails, conferences, hearing documents or used to simply prove you made a contact, attempted to contact, or left a message. Some parents will forget and say you did *not* let them know pertinent information about their children. Then, you can say things like, "Oh, you must have forgotten.

File Organization

I called on Thursday, Feb. 15th at 2:00 PM and talked with your sister, Mary, who said you were at the grocery store, and she would give you the message," or "I called yesterday morning about 9:00 and left you a voicemail." This kind of response can really take the wind out of their sails, and you will get all kinds of apologies!

2. Keep a "To-Do *Folder*."

When you become an administrator, there will be a great deal of paperwork and communication pieces that you will need to handle in a timely manner. So, let's start with the paperwork. When you were a teacher, you thought you had a lot of paperwork, right? You had papers to grade, communication pieces back and forth to the parents, and paperwork for the counselors, psychologists, school administrators, district officials and state officials. You had testing materials, substitute plans, lesson plans, textbook records and so on. If you are like me, I thought there was *no way* paperwork could be anywhere near the amount I had to deal with in the classroom. "After all," I thought, "When I am an administrator, I will have my own office

Wisdom Is the *Principal* Thing!

to do my work, I can close the door when I need to do so, and I will not be *directly* responsible for supervising students all day, so… No Problem." Not so! You will drown and become ineffective in your job as an administrator unless you immediately have organizational skills in place. I am sure you are familiar with the To-Do *Lists*. Well, I used an organizational technique that I called my "To-Do *Folder*," which I actually carried over from the classroom. Of course, the classroom "To-Do Folder" did not have *nearly* as much to do in it as the administrative folder did! You may already be using this technique; however, note the following for possible new tips:

➤ Start with the journalists' questions to prepare to implement the "To-Do Folder" strategy.
- What is the content of the information you have?
- Who sent it and who needs to see it (students, parents, staff and community personnel, district personnel)?
- Where does this information need to go (filed, signed and returned)?

File Organization

- When does this action item need to be done (time frame or deadline)?
- Why is this important (new policies to be implemented, staff allotments for the year)?
- How will I deal with it? How will I structure the action I need to take (delegate it and to whom, or call a meeting about it)?

➤ Place these types of papers in the "To-Do Folder" on your desk:
  - Things that need a response (Memos, letters, phone messages taken from office staff, staff requests, or answer to Red Team's proposal)
  - Things to sign (Budget forms, teacher evaluations, audit forms)
  - Things to do (Action steps that must be taken by you or others)
  - Things that need to be read and distributed to staff members (emails, memos) concerning policy changes for testing requirements and exceptional children or new safety and security measures, as well as many other communications.

Wisdom Is the *Principal* Thing!

I also would arrange papers in my folder by placing information in the front or back in order to prioritize how soon things needed to be addressed. You can also number and color code things with highlighters or colored post-it notes.

3. Keep a "To-Be-Filed Folder."

This is short and sweet. This is a file folder where you place all of the things that have been addressed and can now be filed away for reference later. If you are blessed enough to have your own secretary, he or she will have an efficient way to know what you are ready to have filed.

> ➢ Start with the journalists' questions to prepare to implement a "To-Be-Filed Folder."
>   - What is the content of the information?
>   - Who sent it and who saw it (staff members, parents, students)?
>   - Where does it need to go (notebook or file cabinet drawer)?
>   - When does this need to be done (time frame)?
>   - Why is this important (new policies to be implemented)?

File Organization

- How will I deal with it (file it in notebook or file cabinet drawer, or scan it and send it to a cloud)?

➤ Place these types of papers in the "To-Be-Filed Folder" on your desk:
- Things to which you have responded: memos, letters, phone messages, and staff requests
- Things that you signed: budget forms, teacher evaluations, and audit forms
- Things you have already done: Action steps that you or other staff members took that need to be kept for future reference
- Things you have read and have shared for information and awareness such as policy changes, testing requirements, or hard copies of pertinent emails that you need to keep

4. Keep file cabinet and notebook file systems.

Confidentiality will be one of the major determinants for whether to use a file cabinet system or a notebook system. The security of your office furniture will need to be assessed before you make a decision on this. Some file cabinets have a lock and key, and

Wisdom Is the *Principal* Thing!

others do not. Most bookcases are not secure, even though, I suppose you may be fortunate enough to have one of those lighted bookcases, encased in glass that has a lock. Some desks have large drawers that lock and are equipped for file folders. Make a wise decision, accordingly.

> ➢ Start with the journalists' questions to prepare to implement the file cabinet and notebook file systems.
>   - Who does the information concern?
>   - What is the content of the information? Remember confidentiality concerns.
>   - When does the information need to be accessible (on an as need basis or during certain meetings)?
>   - Where does the information need to be kept, and where will it best serve your needs?
>   - Why does the information need to be filed (a reference for the future)?
>   - How accessible does the information need to be? How can it best be used in the future?
>
> ➢ Keep a **file cabinet** system.

File Organization

Keep alphabetized files in file folders for all projects/programs, teacher teams and departments, curriculum elements, extra-curricular activities, and personal conferences with students and/or parents. You can even use dividers for topics and subtopics; for example, you can use a divider for grade levels and all file folders with teacher's names, meeting notes, and lesson plans for that grade level would be behind that particular divider. You can even color code for different departments, grade levels, and subject areas. The visual people will love this!

> Keep a **notebook** system.

I loved the notebook system! I used the notebooks that have a clear plastic pocket on the front and a clear plastic pocket on the side, so I could insert a title page on the front and the side. Every project or program that included forms I needed to keep was in a notebook. Notebooks are especially handy for district requirements and directives! They allow you to file many forms, letters, and memos that you may need for future reference. You can update old information, such as policies, by replacing and tweaking as needed. Now, this requires time to punch holes, which takes more time than slip-

Wisdom Is the *Principal* Thing!

ping something in a file that is in a file cabinet. I liked it because notebooks are more visible and allow more space for forms to be maintained in an orderly manner, rather than file folders, which become more pliable and much weaker as too many pages are added, destroying the strength of the folder. Of course, in file cabinets things can slide out, get stuck on the bottom of the file drawer, or fall over behind the drawer, only to be found the next year. My secretaries loved the notebook system because I would place things that had been read and addressed in my "To-Be-Filed Folder," and they would place the papers in the appropriate notebook. At the secondary level, student office assistants can file your information that is *not* confidential.

If you are wondering whether to use the notebook system or the file cabinet system, you can use ***both***. Use the notebook system for information that is not sensitive: Updated policies, department or team information, and special programs such as inventory, master scheduling, substitutes, extended day, and transportation. Use the file cabinet system for things that need to be kept confidential: teacher and other staff member conferences, parent conferences and

File Organization

complaints, staff evaluation forms, student records, and other sensitive information.

5. Keep making lists.

   I was once told a story of a principal who had a very hard day, when everything that could go wrong seemed to or actually did. At the end of the day, she threw her hands up, balled up her fists and said, "I don't know who in the world is in charge around here because it certainly is *not* me!"
   You will have days where you will feel just like this. So, I say, "Don't make a fist. Make a list!" This technique was invaluable to me!
   I was always jotting things down. When things are coming at you so fast, and you feel like you are going to lose it, make a list of what needs to be done. Don't just run around and try to do them all because it will be like the tail wagging the dog. There will be no order. Jot down the things that are coming at you that need to be done. When you get a moment, sit down and take a big breath. Calm down! Look at what you have jotted down, and start to structure it by combining, deleting, and prioritizing. When you get up, you will at least *have a plan,* and you

Wisdom Is the *Principal* Thing!

won't just run around like Henny Penny who thought the sky was falling! You can even put notes in your "To-Do Folder." If you are good at making notes in your color note application or another application, use it. Sometimes, I could call the secretary on the radio (if it was not sensitive information) and ask her to jot something down and put it on my desk. That was a *long* time ago. These days, you have the good fortune to whip your phone out and jot a note very quickly or use your voice recorder. Just do what is easier and most efficient for you. People would say, "How do you remember all of that stuff?" "You have such a good memory." My lists helped me to remember and keep some order and structure to my day without going crazy. Remember, if you don't have a plan for your day, your day will plan *for* you. It's a fact. So, I say again: *Don't make a fist. Make a list!*

6. Keep contacts with your files.

 You need a list of contacts that includes every person you may need to contact for every project or program you oversee or with which you may be involved. I always kept my list of contacts with the folder or notebook that included

File Organization

the information concerning that particular responsibility. Once I supervised or coordinated something, I had a notebook or file with every single thing I did and every person I needed to contact to help make the program successful. So, if my principal said, "Kathy, you are in charge of Summer School again this summer," I did not have to become stressed out and try to remember what I did that was effective or ineffective, or which contact I asked to help me. I had it all in one place. Many times, all I had to do was update the student and staff member's names and contact information, and update the program dates and the times!

7. Make a wise decision when deciding whether to keep hard copy files or technological files, if you have a choice. Many applications are popular now, but, as emphasized, decide what is best for *you*.

FOLLOW-THROUGH

1. Give yourself a date to have all information filed within a certain time frame.
2. Keep your files up to date. Don't have so many items in your "To-be-Filed Folder" that the cab-

inet and notebook files are not current. In all files, keep the most current information and discard the old.
3. Limit the number of tasks that you will allow to remain in your "To-Do Folder." Say to yourself, "I will have no more than ten tasks to do." This will help you to continually address things in your folder, so you will have no more than the number you set as a goal.

A Special Note to the Millennium Generation:

I know I am from the "old school" generation. This is a special note to the Millennium Generation. Being technologically efficient and keeping everything on your computers, tablets and cell phones is convenient and great when they are available and work. You can develop and maintain electronic documents, folders, and calendars, and you can store information in technological clouds; however, if the system is down, or has a glitch; if a virus attacks; or if somebody hacks the system, you could lose all of your information. The time may come when you will be glad if you have kept *some* of your information in hard copy form.

My daughter was a junior in high school and kept *everything* in her phone. I tried to tell her she needed

File Organization

to keep a hard copy of at least some due dates of major assignments in a planner. She would not listen. One day, she was running to catch the bus after school. As she ran across the bus parking lot, she dropped her phone. When she realized it, and turned to run back and get it, another bus ran right over it. Every piece of information she needed was in that phone. Her class assignments, due dates, Cultural Choir rehearsals, band practices, National Honor Society events, Student Council meetings and community service events were all gone in a matter of seconds with one "*CRUNCH!*"

You decide. It's your choice. Electronic applications, folders and documents are great. You can use Google or other apps for your calendars too. I use some of them; however, I still keep hard copies of *some* things. If you keep a lot of information in your phone, at least link your applications to Dropbox, Google Drives, iClouds, etc. on your computer, tablet, or laptop, or simply email pertinent information to yourself to store later.

Typical school districts have many types of forms to be used, disseminated, filed, or returned, so it is expected that those documents, which are *already* in hard copy form, will need to be addressed and filed. However, even if something *significant* was sent to me in an email, I would print it and place it in the

Wisdom Is the *Principal* Thing!

appropriate notebook or folder file where it could be easily retrieved. A word to the *wise*, always have more than one strategy.

...I heard long ago in the army: Plans are worthless. Planning is everything.

Dwight D. Eisenhower

CHAPTER 13

HANDLING EMERGENCIES

During my years as a teacher and as an administrator, I experienced many emergencies. As a teacher, I was impacted by another teacher at my school who was brutally murdered by her mentally ill son, three students I taught who were killed in an automobile accident on homecoming night, and a principal who passed out from an illness.

As an assistant principal, I was impacted by a teacher who went into convulsions that resulted from an allergic reaction to medicine; a teacher who was killed in an automobile accident; a cheerleader who was flipped in the air during a pyramid formation, wasn't caught, and hit the pavement; an escaped inmate in the area of our school; gang face offs, fights with weapons and serious injuries (including a brain injury); and other types of emergencies.

There is no way to predict what may occur during your years as a school administrator, but you can prepare yourself by being proactive, rather than reactive. To prepare yourself for whatever may come, begin by planning well.

Wisdom Is the *Principal* Thing!

PREPARATION

Use Your Journalists' Questions!

1. **Who** is designated to be a part of the emergency/crisis team?
    - Assistant principal
    - Counselor/Social Worker
    - Department chairperson
    - Grade level chairperson
    - Nurse
    - Person with knowledge of CPR and other medical needs
    - Principal
    - Secretary
    - Security personnel
    - Team leader

2. **What** kind of emergency is it?
    - Assault
        - Physical/Battery
        - Sexual/Rape
    - Bomb threat
    - Bus accident
    - Car accident, involving student/faculty
    - Closing of school
        - Electricity failure

Handling Emergencies

- Lack of water, heat or air
- Snow, ice or flooding
- Viruses or diseases
> Criminal activity in the area of the school
> Dangerous or suspicious person on or around campus
  - Student
  - Teacher
  - Parent
  - Outsider
> Death on campus or death at school-sponsored event
  - Faculty
  - Student
> Death away from campus
  - Faculty
  - Student
> Disaster that is natural
  - Earthquake
  - Fire
  - Flood
  - Hurricane
  - Tornado
> Disaster that is man made
  - Biological weapon

Wisdom Is the *Principal* Thing!

- - Chemical leak or spill
  - Explosion
  - Fire
  - Gas leak
  - Nuclear power plant danger
  - Radiological danger
  - Terrorism
- ➤ Evacuation
  - Bomb threat
  - Fire
  - Explosion
  - Gas or radiation leak
- ➤ Fighting, especially extreme violence including weapons
- ➤ Gang confrontation or other threat
- ➤ Hostage situation/Active shooter
- ➤ Lockdown
- ➤ Media coverage and/or frenzy
- ➤ Medical emergency
  - Mental
    - ✓ Mental breakdown or meltdown
    - ✓ Suicide attempt
    - ✓ Threat of suicide or homicide
  - Physical

Handling Emergencies

- ✓ Allergic reaction
- ✓ Asthmatic reaction
- ✓ Bleeding from an accident or illness
- ✓ Drug overdose
- ✓ Food poisoning
- ✓ Heart Attack or stroke
- ✓ Pandemic or epidemic of viruses or diseases
- ✓ Stroke
- ✓ Other medical emergencies

> Missing student or staff member
> Taking cover
> Weaponry
  - Shooting
  - Stabbing
  - Other serious injury

3. **When** will the emergency be addressed?
   > Prior Preparation
   - Devise and implement procedures, including communication to the 911 dispatchers, superintendent, media and parents.
   - Make supplies and medical kits available in an organized manner.

Wisdom Is the *Principal* Thing!

- Make sure the emergency manual is updated every year and is easily accessible.
- Make sure emergency routes are posted in every classroom, and in other areas of the school, specifically the gym, Multi-Purpose Room, auditorium, Media Center, cafeteria, and all offices
- Select emergency teams.
➢ Prior Training
- Train **all** staff members.
- Teach everyone his or her role in each type of emergency!
➢ Prior Practice
- Have drills for staff members
- Have drills for students
- Have drills for **<u>each</u>** type of emergency
➢ Immediate implementation of outlined procedures that are in the emergency manual, as needed.

4. **Where** will the emergency be addressed?
    ➢ Auditorium
    ➢ Cafeteria

Handling Emergencies

- Classroom
- Closet
- Gym
- Hallway
- Health Room
- Media Center
- Multipurpose Room
- Office Area
- Restroom
- Storage/Equipment Room

5. **Why** will the emergency be addressed in this manner?
    - Directive from supervisor
    - Instinct and/or wisdom
    - Standard Procedure
    - Training

    Why do you need these staff members involved?
    - Assigned supervision/duties
    - Availability
    - Expertise

    Why do you need these students involved?
    - Endangerment
    - Proximity
    - Vulnerability

6. **How** will the school handle emergencies?
    - Closing school

Wisdom Is the *Principal* Thing!

- ➢ Evacuation
- ➢ Lockdown
- ➢ Taking cover in classrooms, closets, hallways, storage rooms, and offices
- ➢ Early Release
  - Parent pickup
  - Bus transportation

Every school district and every school, whether public, charter, or private should have manuals or notebooks with emergency/crisis procedures. These procedures must be available to whoever may need them. Procedures for typical emergencies such as fire drills, tornado or hurricane drills, lockdowns, and evacuations should be placed with every staff member. These can also be a section of the staff handbook. Procedures for less typical emergencies should be available in some way also.

IMPLEMENTATION

Each school, each emergency is different in some way; however, typically, approach emergencies in the following manner:

1. Determine first what kind of emergency is occurring.

Handling Emergencies

2. Determine the needed resources such as medical supply kits and other emergency kits. These supplies should already be available and key people should know *precisely* where they are housed.
3. Provide medical care, if needed.
4. Communicate what is occurring immediately to the police department, medical personnel, and superintendent's office.
5. Alert the emergency team to inform and decide which emergency procedures will best fit the situation, while help is coming.
6. Alert all students and staff members of the situation, but instruct them to withhold releasing of information until everything is verified. In certain situations, cell phone usage should be limited to the emergency team, as much as possible. One call can spread news to the parents and community, causing pandemonium.
7. Suspend class changes by eliminating the bell system, or staggering the bells, if students are to be released by groups.
8. Begin safety procedures: Use a duck-and-cover, a lockdown, an evacuation, or an early release.
9. Communicate to the parents and the community members which emergency procedures are being implemented, once the facts are verified.

Wisdom Is the *Principal* Thing!

Inform parents of early releases with details of where and when students will be released. This can often become quite chaotic, even though every precaution has been taken to ensure safety for all. When parents are afraid for their children, fear can set in, and they will often ignore procedures. It is *imperative* that *you*, as an administrator, stay as calm and as in control as humanly possible. Even if a parent or staff member loses it, *you cannot*!

10. Continue to communicate to students and staff members concerning the most current situations. Emergency procedures should have several options for communications, in case of power outages and/or cell tower damages.
11. Have one designee to release information to the media, *only* with the permission of the superintendent's office, making sure the information is *current* and *accurate*. Emergency procedures should address cell phone usage by staff members and students. It is very understandable that staff and students will want to contact loved ones during moments of crisis; however, false or embellished information to outside sources could complicate the emergency, making it even more dangerous. Proceed with caution!

Handling Emergencies

12. Preserve evidence, if needed, especially if it includes criminal activity and weapons.
13. Document actions and record damages for insurance claims and financial losses.
14. Do not assume the situation is over until the police, fire department, medical personnel and other agency personnel inform you of such.

FOLLOW-THROUGH

1. Activate the procedures for recovering from the crisis by getting everything and everyone in order and back in place after the emergency is over.
2. Contact any other agencies such as social services or human services to follow up with persons that need it.
3. Debrief with the school's emergency team and include input from staff members, students, and parents. A survey that gives an opportunity for suggestions can really help you to address the next emergency situation more smoothly.
4. Debrief with and get feedback from emergency personnel: medical teams, police officers, and fire department officers.

Wisdom Is the *Principal* Thing!

5. Inform personnel in the superintendent's office of the school's recovery status and the follow-through procedures.

Just remember what is critical, so you will be ready when any emergency situation arises: Prior preparations, trainings, drills, communications to key people as well as knowledge of the locations of emergency manuals, supplies and shelter areas. You have seen by the number of recent school shootings that things constantly change. The 2020 Coronavirus/Covid-19 Pandemic also showed us how *much* the world is changing. Whoever thought that "self-quarantine," "social distancing," and "6 feet" would paralyze the world and tragically remind us of how the word "normal" is transforming? Even so, you *must* be as prepared as possible with a thorough, effective plan.

Be proactive.

Stephen Covey

CHAPTER 14

MASTER SCHEDULING

I had been an assistant principal for three years, when my principal decided to transfer to another school. She had been an assistant principal at my school for many years before becoming the principal and felt she needed a new perspective. Okay, point well taken. However, she left the task of doing the master schedule for our school of 1,200 students to *me*. I had watched her do some things and had even helped her do some things, but this was *scary* to me. The new principal was coming from the high school level where, at the time, in our school district, the scheduling was very different, even using different software, so she could not help me. It was quite a summer for me.

Three years later, I transferred from the middle school where I had been an assistant principal for six years to a senior high school. I was glad to find out that I would not be in charge of the master schedule there. I received a call from a dear friend of mine who was an assistant principal at another middle school in the district. She was distraught. The assistant principal who had been in charge of the master schedule there had accepted a position in another

Wisdom Is the *Principal* Thing!

school district. The newly appointed principal, coming from an elementary school, gave my friend the task of doing the master schedule. "I have never done a master schedule before, Kathy. I don't know what to do." Empathizing, I said, "I'll be right there."

It was a large middle school, but we had all but thirty of the students scheduled in eight days! The thirty students who did not schedule had a conflict and would need to be contacted to make a choice between two courses.

Now, there are different schools with different populations of students and varying levels of teacher expertise and credentials. There are different programs, different software, different facilities, and different needs for every school. Needless to say, there is no "one-size-fits-all" plan. However, there are common steps that can be taken to prepare and devise an excellent master schedule.

PREPARATION

There are some foundational elements of every master schedule, whether the school is primary, elementary, middle, senior high, K-8 or any combination of these. When preparing to tackle and design a master schedule for a school, begin with the basics.

Master Scheduling

Use Your Journalists' Questions!

Your journalists' questions will lay the foundation for your master schedule. To prepare, answer the following questions:

1. **Who** will *teach* (teachers and their assistants)?
    - Who has requested what for this coming year?
    - Who is qualified to teach what?
    - Who *is not* willing to teach what?
    - Who *is* willing to teach what?
    - Who needs special consideration?
    - Who needs to be moved to another grade level or curricular area? Who has qualifications for activities such as coaching sports, coaching cheerleaders, or coaching for academic extra-curricular events such as science, math, and debate competitions? Try not to overload a teacher, no matter how qualified she or he is.

    Who needs to *take* classes?
    - Who needs to take which core subjects? Remember the district and the state guidelines.
    - Who needs which elective subjects?

Wisdom Is the *Principal* Thing!

- ➤ Who is requesting particular subjects such as French or Spanish, band or orchestra, and keyboarding or visual arts?

2. **What** is the content?
    - ➤ English, Language Arts, Reading
    - ➤ Foreign Language
    - ➤ Health
    - ➤ History
    - ➤ Math
    - ➤ Performing Arts
    - ➤ Physical Education
    - ➤ Science
    - ➤ Social Studies
    - ➤ Technology
    - ➤ Visual Arts
    - ➤ Vocational

3. **When** will it be taught?
    - ➤ When will classes begin?
    - ➤ When will classes end?
    - ➤ When will students go to electives?
    - ➤ When will students go to homeroom?
    - ➤ When will students go to lunch?
    - ➤ When will students go to recess?
    - ➤ When will students go to the restroom?

Master Scheduling

- When will students leave homeroom?
- When will teachers have classes?
- When will teachers have hall, cafeteria, bus, playground duties, and other outside duties?
- When will teachers have individual planning time?
- When will teachers have lunch time?
- When will teachers have department or team planning time?
- When will the instructional day begin?
- When will the instructional day end?

4. **Where** will it be taught (locations such as buildings, mobile units, wings, floors)?
    - Where will departments be housed? Together or separated?
    - Where will core classes be held?
    - Where will elective classes be held?
    - Where will exceptional students be housed? Will they be in the building or in a mobile unit? Will they be included in regular classes or will they be separated?
    - Where will grade levels be housed? Together or separated?
    - Where will rotations occur?

Wisdom Is the *Principal* Thing!

> ➤ Where will teams be housed?

My second year as a principal, we moved into our new state-of-the-art facility where the 8th grade building, gym and athletic fields were ***not*** completed. We had to find spaces in the administration building, the 6th and 7th grade buildings, and the elective class halls to hold classes for over 400 students who had no building.

To keep the eighth graders from feeling homeless, we worked really hard to spread the wealth, so to speak. We cleared out big storage rooms and placed desks and chairs in them and rotated classes in and out for all grade levels. We rotated classes into classrooms when other teachers were on their planning periods, used parts of the media center, and used the multipurpose room, so students would not have to always attend class in a storage room.

It was balanced, so one grade level of teachers and students did *not* have to feel lost or less than the others for almost a semester. There will sometimes be challenges when it comes to space and resources too. The key is to make sure no teacher or student feels ignored or neglected.

5. **Why** are you structuring the schedule this way?
    Why do you need this element of the schedule?

Master Scheduling

Why are these students requesting French versus Spanish, chorus versus orchestra, or theatre arts versus keyboarding?
- Academic levels of students (remedial, on grade level, advanced such as gifted, Advanced Placement, and International Baccalaureate)
- Class load requirements with district assignments for teacher/pupil ratios
- English Language Learners
- Exceptionalities such as autism, learning or behavioral disabilities
- Federal guidelines
- Graduation guidelines
- Promotion guidelines
- Parent requests
- Student requests
- State guidelines
- Teacher allotments (number of teachers and teacher assistants allotted for your school)
- Teacher requests

6. **How** exactly will the schedule be designed?
    - Number of classes of each subject
        - Number of required subjects
        - Number of elective subjects

Wisdom Is the *Principal* Thing!

- ➢ Class meeting schedules
  - Daily
    - ✓ Not blocked
      - 45 Minutes
      - 50-90 Minutes
  - Every other day such as an A/B schedule
    - ✓ Blocked
      - One and a half class periods
      - Two class periods
- ➢ Total virtual learning or alternate between in person and virtual times

How will you challenge advanced students and address remedial needs?

- ➢ How will you rotate student groups?
  - Abilities
  - Curricular needs
  - Skill levels
- ➢ How will you prioritize elective requests, especially when your teacher allotments have been reduced?
- ➢ How will you deal with seniors who do not need a full day of courses to graduate? Will they be allowed to leave early, go to work, attend a con-

Master Scheduling

> current enrollment college program, or will they be placed in courses they do not want?
>
> ➢ How will you deal with exceptional students who have misbehaved and have used their allotted days for suspensions, according to federal and state guidelines? Where are you going to put them? How will you deal with this? Don't wait until it happens to decide.

How will you keep records?

IMPLEMENTATION

Once you have collected all of the needed information from your registration sheets, use it to begin your task of scheduling each student to be assigned to a staff member every minute of the school day. Every teacher should be assigned to supervise students except during his or her planning time or lunch time.

1. Begin to enter each student and teacher's information into the computer to start.
2. Use student and parent prioritized requests for electives.

Wisdom Is the *Principal* Thing!

3. First, make sure there are enough teachers to teach the required subjects. Next, consider electives.
4. Create enough sections of every subject to satisfy the requirements. Next, create sections for elective course requests.
5. Create additional sections of classes as needed, if you have enough teachers to teach them. Students may have to be given their second and third choices for electives. You may also combine some courses.
6. Check for conflicts in schedules, especially if the computer will not schedule a student. For example, if the student has requested French, but he also needs an advanced math that is only taught that period, you may have to talk to the student about taking math that period and taking French later.
7. Keep readily accessible records. Obviously, in this day and age, we have clouds, removable drives, and software, so we can enter data into the computer for storage. Wonderful! However, you need to have hard copies of what you enter into the computer. I used grade level notebooks with the student registration sheets and teacher or parent requests. Usually, there are certain consistencies in curriculum across grade levels

because of district and state guidelines, so I highly recommend grade level structuring. Note in some way what you are entering into the computer. Printouts can be cumbersome, especially at the large schools, so you decide how much you can keep. I do recommend a printout at certain stages of data entry, just in case information is lost, there is a glitch in the system, or any other technological issue arises. Notebooks, folders and other kinds of hard copies can save the day, if there is ever a technological problem.

FOLLOW-THROUGH

Even when the master schedule for your school has been completed, follow through by double and triple checking everything. Make sure of the following:

1. Every student is scheduled effectively and has all of the courses he or she is required to take.
2. The teachers and their assistants are scheduled effectively, according to their knowledge, experience, and licensure/certification.
3. The students are scheduled to take whatever they need. Consider grade levels and test scores.

Wisdom Is the *Principal* Thing!

4. The students are scheduled, so ability levels will be addressed and enhanced.
5. The students are scheduled, so at least one to two of their requests are included. It is so disappointing to get *nothing* that you requested.
6. The parent's requests are addressed. Whether you can accommodate them or not, communicate with the parents.
7. The length of all of the class periods is within guidelines. Consider different types of schedules such as A/B Days and virtual learning.
8. The number of minutes between classes is sufficient for orderly transitions between them.
   There is just enough time (not too much) between class periods to eliminate opportunities for shenanigans but never so little time that the teachers and students become frustrated. Frustration leads to other complications.
9. The numbers, genders, racial make-ups, ability levels, special needs, and discipline concerns are balanced among the classes. Do not allow any teacher to have more than his or her fair share of challenges. Balance your schedule out, even if it has to be continued after the first day of school. Your teachers will love you for being fair and for caring enough to make sure *everyone* has a great year.

Master Scheduling

10. The teacher groups such as grade levels, teams, and departments are given opportunities to plan together as much as possible.
11. Some teachers and counselors can take a look at the final schedule to possibly catch something you did not see.
12. A back-up plan or alternative plan is ready for glitches in the schedule the first day. Have the counselors and other personnel on standby to adjust schedules as needed. You can extend homeroom type classes to do adjustments. This will give the teachers time to do "get to know you" type activities anyway.

Your master schedule will determine how effectively your program will operate. Include the foundational elements when creating it, and watch one of the most critical components of curriculum positively impact your school.

Happy Scheduling!

Do what you can, with what you have, where you are.

Theodore Roosevelt

CHAPTER 15

NEW TEACHER SUPPORT

Teachers who are brand new to teaching or teachers who are new to a district, state, or school need support. Even an experienced teacher may have challenges adjusting to a new school, a new principal or assistant principal, or a new situation such as a new teaching assignment. It is your responsibility to help them to adjust and be successful and effective at your school. This is not always easy; however, you will find it less challenging for you if you use these recommendations, many of which can also apply to staff members in other types of positions.

PREPARATION

Use Your Journalists' Questions!

New Teachers Need to *Know* Six Things:

1. **What** they need to do
2. **Who** they need to do it for or who they need to do it with (not grammatical)
3. **When** they need to do it
4. **Where** they need to do it

5. **Why** they need to do it
6. **How** they need to do it

New Teachers Need to *Have* Six Things:

1. **P**hysical Needs that Are Met
2. **O**rder in School Operations
3. **P**rotection from Motivation Killers
4. **I**nstruction, Continually
5. **A**ssociation with Other Staff Members
6. **C**onsistent Expectations

So, learn the acronym **POPIAC** (pronounce it, pah—pee—ak) to help you to remember what all new staff members need.

IMPLEMENTATION

1. **Physical Needs That Are Met**

   Remember Maslow's Hierarchy of Needs that traced a chain of needs from the most basic to the transcendent? Physiological was the foundational level of Maslow's hierarchy: Food, water, shelter, and warmth. It's true. Make sure their basic needs are met. Take the time to see if you

New Teacher Support

need to assist new teachers with any of the following:

> - Finding a place to stay
> - Finding transportation (I have helped to match teachers for carpooling.)
> - Finding the best route to avoid traffic on the way to your school
> - Finding a roommate (I have introduced new teachers who expressed the need for a roommate.)
> - Finding room in the school budget for additional supplies. New teachers are often young, right out of college, and lacking extra money for adding resources to help them in their classrooms.

I have even talked with mothers and fathers of new teachers, or some who were new to the city, and told their parents I would look out for their child! Yes, they are adults, but it is unsettling for some parents when their child leaves home to go to another city or state to teach. It's okay to chat with parents of new teachers and assure them you care about their child's well-being, not just about filling a teaching position. Some school districts will have personnel to do some of this (new teacher support and relocation packages); however, some districts will not. Obviously, private schools and charter schools may not have district resources to help with relocations or new teacher issues, so get ready! Yes, this job will cause you to wear many hats, but physical needs must be met for new staff members to have a successful experience.

2. **Order in School Operations**

You must operate your school in an orderly manner for a new teacher to feel comfortable and experience success. It must be structured so that all staff members and students are in their assigned places at the assigned times and doing what they are assigned to do. This may sound simplistic, but new teachers feel supported when the following occurs:
- People they need are available.
- Policies and procedures are in place and stable.
- Resources they need to teach effectively are available.
- Schedules and plans for classes and other elements of school operations are clearly outlined and in place.

New Teacher Support

> Whatever and whoever they need is not only in place and available, but *easy* to access. A new teacher is going to become very frustrated if he or she needs to talk with the school counselor about a student, for example, and the counselor is almost always unavailable.

3. **Protection from Motivation Killers**

We don't like to talk about it, but there are those who will kill the passion, excitement, zeal and creativity of the new teacher in a skinny minute. They can be other teachers who really do not want to be at the school for one reason or another or uncooperative parents who try to make everything that is not right with their children the fault of the school. Whatever the root of this tendency to kill someone else's motivation happens to be, you have to do whatever you can to protect all of the new teachers from it. Safety is also in Maslow's hierarchy. Address toxic behavior and protect them from the following:

> Being over-whelmed from too many expectations at once

Wisdom Is the *Principal* Thing!

> - Having to depend on outside help because the school is not providing what they need
> - Working with frustrated and depressed teachers who bring their ill feelings and troubles from home to work
> - Discouraging, intimidating, or bullying teachers
> - Fixating students who think it's cute to go the extra mile to make things hard and extra challenging for the teacher that they *know* is new
> - Intimidating community members or parents
> - Jaded, cynical, veteran teachers who are often jealous of the new teacher's excitement

4. **Instruction, Continually**

New teachers need to be given formal and informal trainings. Continual learning can enhance a teacher's confidence and self-esteem, which is another of Maslow's levels. Continual learning will promote growth, which in turn will positively impact students.

New Teacher Support

- ➢ Provide opportunities for formal trainings:
  - Department Level
  - School Level
  - District Level
  - State or National Level
- ➢ Provide opportunities for informal trainings:
  - Mentor and buddy teacher times to plan together
  - Observations of other teachers
  - Observations of teacher coaches
  - Risk-free and supportive observations by another teacher, by an administrator, and by a curriculum facilitator

5. **Association with Other Staff Members**

New teachers need to feel that their colleagues and supervisors care. They need to feel like they belong. Maslow insisted on this, and I have also found it to be true. Teachers will not stay if they do not feel loved and a part of something great. Put these strategies in place:

- ➢ Assign a Mentor/Buddy Teacher.

Wisdom Is the *Principal* Thing!

> - Assign to a small team, department or grade level group.
> - Provide opportunities for them to get to know other staff members.
>   - Mingle, chat, and snack times on teacher workdays
>   - Staff member fun times at the school with cook outs, pot luck, and covered dish lunches on work days or special occasions
>   - Staff member fun times away from the campus. Have retreats, go bowling, and eat at restaurants. Get away!
>   - Warm-up activities, brief games, snacks, mingling, and lots of *fun* at the faculty meetings. Yes, you have business to do, but keep them connecting and laughing, and you will have more success keeping them happy, as long as the *other* elements are in place!

6. **Consistent Expectations**

New teachers must have consistency in *all* aspects of the job. Ineffectiveness, poor communication,

New Teacher Support

chaos and disorder will cause new teachers to start looking at the many *available* options. They must find consistency in these daily operations:

- Curriculum expectations
- Day-to-Day operations such as bells, announcements, and assemblies
- Disciplinary actions by administrators for staff and students
- Duty stations
- Policies (federal, state, and district)
- Procedures
  - Arrival/Dismissal of students
  - Emergency situations
  - Health needs
  - Lunch/Cafeteria
  - Memos, emails, website info
  - Observations and evaluations
  - Opening and closing of school
  - Playground/other outside areas
- Schedules
  - Attendance submissions
  - Grade submissions/report cards
  - Progress reports
  - Meetings such as faculty, team, grade level, department, PTA/PTO

Wisdom Is the *Principal* Thing!

7. **Things you *don't* want to do**

   Administrators should avoid certain assignments that can discourage even the most passionate teacher. Note the following things you should never do:
   - Don't give a new teacher a floating schedule of classrooms in which to teach.
   - Don't give a new teacher the most challenging students (whether discipline or special needs) At least, try to limit the number.
   - Don't give a new higher-level teacher more than two preparations: one, if possible.
   - Don't assign a new teacher, if possible, extra-curricular activities unless he or she specifically asks for it. Don't allow him or her to supervise more than one task at a time. New teachers are very excited at first, and sometimes, they bite off more than they can chew! It will help if you get requests in writing, in case the need to have a discussion comes later.

New Teacher Support

- ➢ Don't assign a new teacher to work closely with teachers that you *know* are weak and are ineffective, academically, socially or disciplinarily.
- ➢ Don't assign a new teacher to work closely with other teachers who are negative or who not only foster discontentment but also foster dissention among others.

8. **Things you *do* want to do**

Administrators should provide opportunities for new teachers to be successful, to stay content, and to remain encouraged. They should be proactive and not wait until complaints arise or until a new teacher loses it.

- ➢ Assign a mentor or buddy teacher with the following qualities:
  - Has years of experience but *fondly* remembers what it was like to be a new teacher
  - Is familiar with guidelines and is familiar with resources for the school, district, and state
  - Has an outstanding work ethic

Wisdom Is the *Principal* Thing!

- *Wants* to be a mentor and is very willing to share his or her knowledge and expertise
- Is very positive, has integrity, and knows how to get the job done, even during times of obstacles and challenges
- Is teachable and can teach others, effectively
- Is able to see the humor in situations. A merry heart is excellent medicine for everyone! Teaching them to find humor in their daily situations can make the difference when it comes to retaining a new teacher.

➢ Have a new teacher orientation for your school, even if your district has one too. Personalize it.

➢ Have an open-door policy for them. Remember to be sensitive and empathic to emergencies and struggles that may arise. A divorce, a break up with a significant other, a medical issue, or the death of a loved one are some of the events that must be met with compassion. Yes, job performance is very important, but supporting

New Teacher Support

and helping them to get *through tough situations* is important too. Compassion helps to build relationships that result in loyalty.

➤ Introduce them to key personnel.
➤ Make certain they understand evaluation procedures for new personnel and what your school and state's expectations are.
➤ Take them or have a positive staff member to take them on a tour of the school (can be the buddy teacher) and include the following:

- Administrative offices and other areas for principal and assistant principals
- Art areas (visual, graphic, performing)
- Bus lot
- Cafeteria
- Copy room
- Counseling department
- Fields for organized sports
- Foreign language area
- Gathering areas for the older students (malls, quads, patios, etc.)
- Gym
- Main office

Wisdom Is the *Principal* Thing!

- Media Center
- Parent drop-off/pick-up area
- Play areas
- Restrooms
- Secretaries' offices (especially financial, attendance, and records) and the principal's secretary
- Their classrooms - How about a gift on their desks?
- Their grade level, department, or team areas

FOLLOW-THROUGH

1. Find a way to check on the new teachers without intimidating them. Your knowledge of their status cannot come from observations and evaluations or from hearsay alone.
    - Chat with them in the hallway.
    - Chat with them at lunch time.
    - Chat with them before and after the school day.
    - Chat with them during their planning time (briefly because they may have much to do).
2. Ask how they *personally* are doing.

New Teacher Support

3. Ask how things are going in their classes.
4. Ask them if there is anything *you* personally need to check.
5. Pay attention!
    - Do they seem content?
    - Do they seem angry?
    - Do they seem frustrated?
    - Do they seem afraid?
    - Do they seem confused?
    - Do they seem to be comfortable with the kids?
    - Are they forming good relationships with other staff members or are they loners?
    - Do they look you in the eye when they talk with you, or do they look away and appear uncomfortable? If so, something is amiss!
    - Are they going in the right direction? Is it the path to effectiveness and success?
6. Find a way to learn how new teachers are doing and address it! Although much of this information can be used for supporting *all* teachers and even staff members in other positions, you <u>*must*</u> take care of the new ones.

Wisdom Is the *Principal* Thing!

New teachers can be inundated with much information and many expectations at once. I have seen some beginning teachers with so much potential throw in the towel because they felt it was too much, especially for the pay! Remember what they *need to know*, remember what they *need to have*, and remember the acronym ***POPIAC***. Then, instead of seeing new teachers with great potential give up, you will see new teachers with great potential blossom!

A strategic leader can provide direction and vision, motivate through love, and build a complementary team based on mutual respect if he is more effectiveness-minded than efficiency-minded, more concerned with direction and results than with methods, systems, and procedures.

Stephen Covey

CHAPTER 16

OBSERVATIONS AND EVALUATIONS

Observation and evaluation of teachers and other staff members can be a very sensitive subject. Those being observed are usually a bit intimidated about being observed, especially when it is a formal observation that is part of the evaluation process. Often, they are *not* glad to see you come and are *very* glad to see you go. You need to develop a relationship with your staff members, so they will know that you are *not* there to *catch them doing something wrong*.

They need to be convinced that your purpose when you observe is to *help them* to be as effective as possible at what they are expected to do. You are not there to criticize but to acknowledge the areas in which they are the most effective and to give recommendations for the areas in which they could use some improvement. They need to know the observation process is not going to be used as a weapon for leverage or causing fear but a tool and a resource to help them and their students. Assure them that you are willing to do everything in your power to make their teaching experience the best that it can possibly be. The answers to the pertinent questions below will help structure your observation and evaluation plans.

Wisdom Is the *Principal* Thing!

PREPARATION

Use Your Journalists' Questions!

1. **Who** needs to be observed?
    - Counselors
    - Curriculum specialists such as literacy, math, and other facilitators
    - Staff members who are non-certified
    - Staff members who represent specialty areas such as psychologists, nurses, social workers, and teachers of English Language Learners and special needs students
    - Teachers approaching tenure
    - Teachers in a certain curricular area
    - Teachers in a department
    - Teachers on a grade level or team
    - Teachers who are new to teaching in the state, who are new to teaching a subject, or who are new to teaching on a grade level

2. **What** content/subject, class, or grade level will be observed?
    - What would you like for teachers to do when you walk into their rooms?

Observations and Evaluations

- Give you a copy of all handouts and other materials
- Include you in the activities
- Proceed with the class instruction as if you were not present

➢ What is your policy on parents observing teachers (appointment only or open door)? This can get quite complicated, depending upon the motives of the observers.

3. **Where** do you need to observe?
   ➢ Cafeteria
   ➢ Classroom
   ➢ Gymnasium
   ➢ Lab
   ➢ Outside (playground, ball fields)
   ➢ Media Center
   ➢ Multi-purpose room
   ➢ Technology classroom

4. **When** do you need to observe?
   ➢ Frequency during a quarter, semester, session or year (following guidelines)
   ➢ Morning or afternoon
   ➢ Time of day such as class times

Wisdom Is the *Principal* Thing!

5. **Why** do you need to observe?
    - Curricular issues, disciplinary issues, or parent complaints
    - District or state requirements
    - Requests by teachers

6. **How** do you need to observe?
    - Announced observations
    - Full class observations
    - Partial class observations
    - Unannounced observations
    - Walk-through observations, 5 to 10 minutes with immediate feedback by form, email, or note

IMPLEMENTATION

1. Be knowledgeable of federal, state, district and school guidelines.
2. Inform staff members who are assigned to be observed by you what your procedure for observing will be, including the following:
    - Will observations be unannounced or announced?
    - Will a copy of every observation be given to the staff member?

Observations and Evaluations

- ➢ Will a conference be required after certain observations or after every observation?
- ➢ Will every observer be included in the evaluation process?
- ➢ Will a signature be required after every observation or certain observations?
- ➢ May a teacher or other staff member invite you to observe and evaluate during a special presentation?

3. Give written feedback, even if it is just a note or an email after a brief visit.
4. Set a conference after a *formal* observation.
5. Have the conference as soon as possible following the evaluation, while everyone's memory is fresh. Details will be forgotten as time passes.
6. Allow the teacher or other staff member to have input during the conference concerning what he or she feels is needed to be more effective in the assigned position.
7. Summarize the conference in writing if further action is required. Most school districts have conference evaluation forms that the administrator and staff member can sign. Additionally, have in writing what the future actions will be for all participants, according to what needs to be done.

Wisdom Is the *Principal* Thing!

FOLLOW-THROUGH

1. Do informal observations (walk-throughs) to see how the teacher is doing, especially if the teacher needs to improve some areas of classroom instruction or classroom management.
2. Conduct at least one formal observation in order to observe the whole picture. Some states may require more.
3. Keep any promises you made during a conference to provide additional support.
    - Additional supplies
    - Additional curricular materials
    - Help with classroom management and disciplinary concerns
    - Help with instructional techniques
    - Help with parent complaints
    - Help with supervision of duty stations
    - Help with extra-curricular duties
4. Ask the teacher to invite you to observe a special presentation by him or her.
5. Have another teacher of the same subject area to help, if needed, by being available to provide support in these ways:
    - Observing each other
    - Planning together
    - Supporting, however needed

Observations and Evaluations

If you develop a trusting relationship with your teachers and with other staff members, they will be happy to *invite* you to observe them working with students. It can become the most encouraging portion of their day and yours too!

Think win-win.

Stephen Covey

CHAPTER 17

OPENING AND CLOSING THE SCHOOL YEAR

My first year as a principal was quite challenging. I only had 250 students, but we were to operate our middle school in one wing of a new elementary school that was being built. Our new middle school, which would hold 1,000 *additional* students, was also under construction. I had to open a new school while overseeing the construction of both schools. So, actually, for two consecutive years, I opened a new school! Talk about nerve racking!

The first year, the main office of the building of the elementary school where we were housed had not been constructed yet, so we had to be creative. The room that we made our main office was the size of a walk-in closet. In fact, it probably *was* a closet! Well, we were hustling and bustling around doing all of the things needed to open school in two weeks, and I came into our main office for something. A tall, hefty man, who had made a delivery to the school, was standing in the office with his hand over his mouth, trying not to burst out laughing. I asked him what was so funny. "You better not try to fit four people in here!" he drawled, just cracking up. I could

Wisdom Is the *Principal* Thing!

not do anything but laugh too! "Hey, you use what you have, right?" This is what administrators have to do. Don't focus on what you don't have! Use what you have, smile, and keep moving. How you open a school will impact the current school year, and how you close a school will impact the next school year.

OPENING THE SCHOOL YEAR

PREPARATION

Use Your Journalists' Questions!

When opening the school for a new year, everyone needs to know the answers to six questions.

1. **Who** is in charge of each area of responsibility? **Who** should I collect equipment, materials, and keys from to use?
2. **What** equipment or materials can I collect?
3. **When** can I collect equipment, materials, and keys?
4. **Where** can I collect equipment, materials, and keys?
5. **Why** do I need to keep the equipment, materials, or keys in a particular place?
    ➤ Accessibility

Opening and Closing the School Year

- Security
6. **How** do I need to obtain equipment, materials, or keys?
    - District procedures
    - School procedures
    - Forms
    - Logs

    How do I get help, if I need it?

IMPLEMENTATION

1. Know the personnel who are in charge of key areas and know their responsibilities. These are typical assignments:
    - Assistant/Vice Principals and Deans
        - Discipline
        - Extended day programs
        - Furniture inventory in the classrooms and other areas
        - Maintenance
        - Safety and crisis management
        - Student transportation
        - Substitutes
        - Teacher classroom and grade level assignments
        - Teacher orientations and trainings

Wisdom Is the *Principal* Thing!

- Teacher observations and teacher evaluations
- Testing
- Counselors
  - School records
  - Promotion and retention lists
  - Individual education plans
  - Individual and group counseling files
  - Student placement
- Curriculum Specialists
  - Curriculum to be distributed and stored
  - Resource guides
  - Supplemental curriculum (preparation for testing)
- Department Chairpersons
  - Textbooks
  - Teacher manuals
  - Supplemental materials
- Media Specialists
  - Audio-visuals and other media
  - Books
- Technology Specialists
  - Computers
  - Other electronic devices

Opening and Closing the School Year

- School websites

2. Open the school year with an orientation and discuss procedures.
3. Make sure all teachers and other staff members have the following information, preferably in a staff handbook:
   - Attendance sheets and procedures for recording student attendance
   - Bell and class change times
   - Bus and bus lot rules for students
   - Cafeteria expectations--Use soft voices (6-inch voices), leave areas clean, don't skip in front of others in line.
   - Calendar of teacher workdays, leave days, school days, vacation days, and make-up days.
   - Class lists with student and parent information such as mail and email addresses, and phone numbers for work and home
   - Contact information sheet, requesting staff members' names, mailing addresses, telephone numbers, email addresses, and licensure/certification information
   - Copy of the master schedule, including teaching assignments by teams, departments, classrooms, and grade

Wisdom Is the *Principal* Thing!

levels. Include times for personal planning and classroom preparation.
- Daily schedule with class times, arrival/departure times, and lunch/break times for students and teachers
- Designated student areas for gathering times before school, after school, during lunches, and during breaks
- Discipline procedures and the referral forms to be used
- Dress code for teachers and students, including uniform policies, if applicable.
- Duty schedules for staff members before and after school and during class changes, whether in the hallways, bus lot, parking lot, cafeteria, outside, and other gathering areas
- Emergency procedures (evacuations, weather and active shooter drills, and lockdowns)
- Food procedures – Breakfast, lunch and snack times (cafeteria involvement?)
- General procedures (communication, parking, and locations of handbooks and manuals)

Opening and Closing the School Year

> ➤ Information for counselors, itinerant and other key staff members,
> ➤ Lists of do's and don'ts for reviewing with students during the first day of school. Examples are as follows:
>   - Follow the directions of all staff members.
>   - Settle all differences peacefully or tell a staff member.
>   - Respect the rights and property of others. Respect school property.
>   - Walk quietly. Don't run.
>   - Use no profanity or vulgarities.
>   - Use appropriate words ("Yes," "No," "Thank you," "Excuse me," and "Please") Be polite.
>   - Do not show bad attitudes with inappropriate behavior (muttering, ignoring staff members, turning your back or walking away from them, sucking teeth, rolling eyes, shrugging shoulders)
>   - Keep your hands, feet and objects to yourself.

Wisdom Is the *Principal* Thing!

- Be at the right place, at the right time, which is on time.
- Location of keys to rooms, offices, and storage areas
- Major test days for secondary schools (Define the *difference* between a major test and a quiz!)
- Map of the school for teachers who are new to the school
- New teacher support plans, including new teacher orientation information for the district and the school.
- No tolerance policies, including the use of weapons, alcohol, and illegal substances. No violence or assaults
- Observation and evaluation procedures and schedules
- Pay schedule dates
- Previous year's yearbook for new teachers to become familiar with the names and faces of other staff members
- Procedures for requesting supplies as well as other resources
- Referral procedures for students who may have special needs

Opening and Closing the School Year

- Responsibility list with duties and assignments for administrators and for other staff members
- Room and office assignments, and rotation of offices for itinerant staff members
- Rosters of students
- Schedule of staff meetings
- Schedule and locations of grade level, department, and team meetings
- School goals with at least five areas of focus for the year. For example, school safety, school climate, student academic achievement, community and school collaboration, and possibly, home/school communication
- School theme, colors, and mascot
- State, federal, and district policies and where to find them
- Substitute teacher procedures
- Technology availability and technology expectations such as maintaining and communicating per the school website
- Trainings (required and optional)

> Transportation procedures for parent drop-off/pick-up and procedures for bus transportation
4. Give opportunities for clarifications and questions that may be needed.

FOLLOW-THROUGH

1. Be accessible.
2. Be supportive.
3. Be visible. (Don't just go into your office and close the door!)
4. Target problems and challenges immediately!
5. Check with leaders in the school to assess the progress and to finalize anything incomplete.

CLOSING THE SCHOOL YEAR

All staff members need some kind of instruction and preparation for *closing* the school year. Make sure, after answering the journalists' questions, each teacher and other staff members return or address these things to help successfully close your school year. Teachers should have a packet with lists that key personnel can sign to indicate that they and other staff members have correctly and have appropriately brought closure to specific areas. For example, the

Opening and Closing the School Year

grade level counselor can sign the checkout sheet when the teacher submits the promotion/retention information for her students. Most schools refer to these as checkout or closing-the-school-year procedures.

PREPARATION

Use Your Journalists' Questions!

When closing the school year, everyone needs to know the answers to pertinent questions for returning, recording, and accountability purposes.

1. **Who** do I return equipment, keys, and materials to for storage?
2. **What** can I keep?
   What do I need to return?
3. **When** do I need to return them?
4. **Where** do I need to return them?
   - ➢ Curriculum storage space
   - ➢ Media center
   - ➢ Office
   - ➢ Technology storage space
5. **Why** do I need to take the equipment, keys, and materials to a particular place?
   - ➢ Accountability

Wisdom Is the *Principal* Thing!

- Inventory
- Security

Why do I need to have my room clear of clutter, information posted on the walls, or things on the floor (summer cleaning, painting)?

6. **How** do I return equipment, keys, or materials?
    - By logging in and out
    - In boxes
    - On Carts
    - With forms

How do I get help if I need it?

IMPLEMENTATION

1. Make sure classrooms and office areas are neat and organized.
    - Remove all articles off the floor because mopping, stripping, waxing, or buffing might be in the plans.
    - Remove all postings from the walls if painting or changes are planned.
2. Make sure keys are secured.
    - Return keys, especially master keys.
    - Secure and identify keys for summer work.
3. Make sure all records are submitted and secured.

Opening and Closing the School Year

- ➢ Administrators
  - Grade books and other records
  - Inventory lists of *all* areas
  - Maintenance requests
  - Repair lists for classrooms, offices, restrooms, and other areas.
  - Technology repair lists
  - Technology requests
- ➢ Counselors
  - Cumulative records
  - Promotion/Retention records
  - Student grade reports
  - Testing results
- ➢ Secretaries
  - Attendance information
  - Promotion/Retention information for parents
  - Receipt books and bank pouches
  - Student financial obligations
- ➢ Teachers
  - Special Education or ELL
    - ✓ Individual Education Plans
    - ✓ Placement recommendations
  - Lead teachers such as team leaders, department chairpersons, and curriculum specialists

Wisdom Is the *Principal* Thing!

- ✓ Supplemental books
- ✓ Standardized assessments, guides, and manuals

4. Make sure resources are returned, which is critical, so resources will not be depleted when school reopens.
    - ➢ Computers, especially lap computers
    - ➢ Audio/visual equipment
    - ➢ Media Center materials, checked out
    - ➢ Supplemental curriculum for storage
    - ➢ Staff handbooks for updating and for redistributing
    - ➢ School supplies: One year, my supervisors collected all of the staplers. They had been disappearing!
    - ➢ Textbooks

5. Make sure personal information is on file.
    - ➢ Intent form for upcoming school year (move, transfer, retire or stay)
    - ➢ Summer address
    - ➢ Summer email
    - ➢ Summer telephone number
    - ➢ Vacation dates
        - • Contacts that concern details or situations from the past year or session may be needed.

Opening and Closing the School Year

- Contacts that concern possibilities for the upcoming school year or session may be needed

FOLLOW-THROUGH

1. Make sure all checkout forms have been submitted and thoroughly completed before staff members leave for the summer.
   Note: Many school systems have online record keeping for student attendance, grade reports, and other information. For example, currently, Power School is a popular student information system being used globally. Teachers, when they checkout, will still need to show evidence that critical information has been entered online by the deadlines.
2. Make sure general information is considered for the upcoming school year.
   - Requests for supervision of an extra-curricular activity
   - Requests for changes in teacher room or subject assignments
   - Requests for teaching Summer School
   - Requests for attending conferences during the summer, at the school's expense
3. Be accessible.

Wisdom Is the *Principal* Thing!

4. Be supportive.
5. Be visible.
6. Have debriefing meetings with targeted school leaders to pinpoint the successes and improvements needed. Surveys may be also used.
7. Target the challenges and potential problems immediately! They will *not* just go away.

Every school is different and staff members will have a variety of responsibilities, depending on the needs of your school. Adjust as necessary the recommendations that have been given, so the opening and closing of your school will go as smoothly as possible.

Begin with the end in mind.

Stephen Covey

CHAPTER 18

PRIORITIZING RESPONSIBILITIES

I will be honest with you. Prioritizing will become harder than you have known it to be in the past. It's true you had much to be concerned about as classroom teachers and counselors, or as personnel in other non-administrative positions; however, it was always very clear that your assigned students must be supervised at all times. This prioritized things *for* you. Other things had to be addressed during your planning time, during your lunch time, or during before or after-school times.

As an administrator, you make choices between upset, yelling and crying parents or parents who want to become involved; screaming, scheming and crying students, or students with wonderful, creative ideas for how to improve the school; crying and burned out or overwhelmed teachers or teachers who want to meet with you about recommendations for improving this year or the next school year; concerns from specialty faculty members such as literacy and math facilitators, itinerant staff such as school nurses or psychologists; concerns from non-certified staff members such as cafeteria personnel, bus drivers, secretaries, or custodians; and concerns from district supervisors about district and state requirements such as testing, safety audits, exceptional children audits, trainings for you as an administrator, and trainings for your staff members. Whew!

Although challenging, prioritizing can be simplified by having a plan and working your plan as much as possible.

PREPARATION

Use Your Journalists' Questions!

1. **Who** needs to be involved in addressing this responsibility?
2. **What** is the most important element of the responsibility at this time?
   What is the purpose behind what needs to be done?
3. **When** must I address this responsibility?
   When do I need to have it resolved?
4. **Where** must I address this responsibility?
   Where does it need to be resolved?
5. **Why** is it the *most important* concern at this time?
   Why is it more important than anything else that needs to be done (*Priority*)?
6. **How** do I approach the responsibility?

Prioritizing Responsibilities

How do I address it?
How do I resolve it?

IMPLEMENTATION

There are many strategies for prioritizing. I'm sure you can find wonderful ideas online, and you may have some strategies that you have already used. However, here is what helped me.

Use the Critical Prioritizing Strategy

1. Crisis (evacuations, weather and shooter drills, lockdowns and other emergencies)
2. Safety/Danger (duty stations manned, kids in appropriate areas, kids supervised at all times). Of course, the amount of freedom that kids have depends on grade levels, maturity levels, concerns about bullying, fights, theft, and so on.
3. State and district requirements such as audits, testing, accreditations and deadlines
4. Parent and teacher concerns
5. Other tasks and responsibilities
6. Student concerns

Wisdom Is the *Principal* Thing!

"Student concerns" are last *only* because numbers 1–5 concern them anyway. Everything we do is for the good of the students. However, if there is a crisis, the last thing you are going to deal with at that moment is a student complaint about not liking the teacher.

Use the Hour-By-Hour Strategy

When I was overwhelmed and had so much to do, I would sometimes do things hour by hour. This, of course, is only feasible if you are not dealing with numbers 1–3 of the "Prioritizing Strategy" because none are concerns or all have been addressed. Start with the closest deadline first in each of the following areas:

1. One hour on testing plans
2. One hour on presentations: to grade level, team, department, and staff meetings; to students in assemblies or in small group meetings; to parents in PTA/PTO organizational meetings or trainings; to district office personnel for budget emergencies, exclusion hearings, or justifications for allotments.

Prioritizing Responsibilities

3. One hour on discipline referrals and concerns
4. One hour on observation and evaluation of teachers and other staff members
5. One hour supervising a lunch period
6. One hour responding to emails/letters or making telephone calls
7. One hour having individual meetings or group conferences
8. One hour addressing items in your "To-Do Folder"

Note what *this* particular strategy will do. It will allow you to make progress on several things instead of just one or two. You know how you start on something, and you are so determined to finish it that you do not accomplish anything else that day? Then, sometimes you don't even finish the one thing you *did* work on that day because you kept being interrupted to address other issues? At least *this* strategy will give you a feeling of accomplishing and making some headway on several things. It's a mentality. You just feel better. It helps eliminate that feeling that you went through the whole day and didn't really accomplish much of anything.

Then, if necessary, something you did not get to do can be placed at the top of your list for the next day.

Wisdom Is the *Principal* Thing!

Even if you do not finish all of these, this will show you that your goal to make progress on several things was accomplished. You did just that.

Use the Subject-By-Subject Strategy

You can use a subject-by-subject strategy by structuring your time by topics. This is very similar to the hour-by-hour strategy, only you will work on that subject from start to finish instead of stopping to work on another topic because the hour is over. Whether you work on that subject two hours or one whole day, you are committed to that project until it is completed, at least as much as possible for that time. Some of you may do well with this, especially if you are the type of person that does not like to have *too* many irons in the fire at one time, so to speak. Now, you *will* have to do *some* multi-tasking. However, at times, you might like to work on something and actually finish it before you take on a new task. The following can be done in any order.

1. Time presenting (As already noted, this will include staff groups, students, or parents.)
2. Time addressing discipline referrals from your teachers and preparing for exclusion and expulsion hearings

Prioritizing Responsibilities

> Referrals should be prioritized by dates and times unless the seriousness of an offense places the referral at the top of the pile.

3. Time conducting teacher observations and evaluations
4. Time supervising areas of the school facilities
5. Time coordinating assemblies, class coverage, inventory, substitutes, transportation, testing schedules, extended day programs, and other typical administrative responsibilities
6. Time responding to emails/letters or making telephone calls
7. Time conducting conferences with parents or staff members
8. Time addressing items in your "To-Do Folder"

Strategies, without a doubt, do vary in effectiveness with different schools, and what works at one school may or may not work at another. The good news is this: There *are* effective strategies that will help you to plan your day.

Wisdom Is the *Principal* Thing!

FOLLOW-THROUGH

1. Try different and creative strategies and decide what works best for you and your school situation.
2. Decide which strategy you will use on different types of days and during different times of the year.
3. Talk with your supervisor or colleague about your performance when it comes to the subject of prioritizing. Be honest and let him or her give you feedback, positive or negative.
4. Pay attention and adjust, *accordingly*, when you receive comments from staff members, students and parents. For example, if a staff member brings to your attention that you are *always* seeing students during her planning period, which makes you unavailable to see her about something, then you would want to move your time slot for seeing students around. You never want to be unavailable to the same group of people at the same time, every day.
5. Don't forget your purpose, which is to ensure all students are educated as effectively as possible. With *all* of your prioritizing,

Prioritizing Responsibilities

> don't lose sight of the vision and mission of the school because they are what will keep you on the right path toward success.

I often used a combination of these strategies. For example, when students were not in school in the summer and on teacher workdays, I liked to use the Subject-by-Subject strategy. I had time and did not have as many interruptions. When students were in school, I used the Critical Prioritizing Strategy or the Hour-by-Hour Strategy, depending on what was occurring at the time. During state testing, the strategy to use would most likely be Subject-by-Subject because this is the topic you will need to focus on for that time. You would stay focused on testing, for the most part, and only move into another strategy if something critical happened such as someone being injured, some student pulling the fire alarm, or some man being seen on campus with a gun! Always, make your schedule, keeping deadlines in mind.

The key is not to prioritize what's on your schedule, but to schedule your priorities.

Stephen R. Covey

CHAPTER 19

STAFF AND VOLUNTEER APPRECIATION

You *must* show appreciation to all of your staff members as well as helpful parents and volunteers. You definitely need to do it on the designated calendar appreciation days for teachers, counselors, nurses and other staff members. Don't forget bus drivers, cafeteria workers, secretaries, custodians, and security personnel. You might want to recognize specific students who have done outstanding things to benefit the school and community. It would also be *wise* to recognize your supervisor on the annual Boss's Day! Have these days marked in advance on your personal calendar and on the school calendar.

PREPARATION

Use Your Journalists' Questions!

1. **Who** should be recognized?
2. **What** should the persons be recognized for doing?
3. **When** should the persons be recognized?
4. **Where** can the persons be recognized?
5. **Why** should the persons be recognized in this manner?

Wisdom Is the *Principal* Thing!

6. **How** would the persons *prefer* to be recognized?

IMPLEMENTATION

1. Plan to recognize these staff members.
   - Administrators
   - Bus drivers
   - Cafeteria workers
   - Coaches and other staff members supervising extra-curricular activities
   - Counselors
   - Curriculum specialists
   - Custodians
   - Itinerate staff members such as nurses, psychologists, and social workers
   - Parents
   - Secretaries
   - Security and school resource officers
   - Students
   - Teachers/Teacher assistants
   - Volunteers
2. Find out how the people working at your school or are connected to your school, would *like* to be recognized.
   - Ask each person, verbally.
   - Survey the group, written or online.

Staff and Volunteer Appreciation

- Ask leaders of the team, grade level or department to which they belong.
- Watch their responses to your efforts to recognize them. Pay attention to verbal and non-verbal responses. If someone appears to be uncomfortable when you pat her or him on the back, don't do it again!

3. Give from the heart. Don't just do something to check it off of your list. People know when you really mean what you are doing.
4. Recognize personnel in a variety of ways.
   - Intercom announcement
   - School newspaper announcement
   - Community news announcement
   - School marquee or banner
   - School website
   - Catered breakfast or prepaid restaurant buffet breakfast
   - Catered lunch or allowing the group to go out to lunch while others cover their duties. I did this for the secretarial staff, especially, to get them away from the school and the phones ringing. A prepaid lunch was *marvelous* to them. Teachers and parents can help during their free time.

Wisdom Is the *Principal* Thing!

- Emails
- Gifts in mail boxes (candy, gift bags with a variety of handy items) Parents love to help with these.
- Gifts or flowers on their desks. Once we placed red poinsettias on the top of the counters in the cafeteria, so all of the cafeteria staff members could take one home for Christmas. They loved it!
- Food in the teacher's lounge: Make it available when they *can* get it.
- Notes in mailboxes or on desks
- Recognitions in staff meetings
- Student notes or drawn pictures
- Your personal and individual verbal recognition of a job well done. Know your staff members. Some people are not comfortable being recognized in front of crowds, but they sure do love a personal fist bump or thumbs-up!

5. Appeal to parents and volunteers to help show appreciation to staff members and students.
6. Appeal to staff members and students to help to show appreciation to parents and volunteers.
7. Use a flier. It can be written or in an email. Here is an example:

Staff and Volunteer Appreciation

Dear **School Name** Bus Driver,

You are invited to have breakfast *on us* at Shoney's on _____ Road at 8:45 AM on Friday, April 22nd in appreciation for all you do for our school's students.

Please come. We are looking forward to your allowing us to do this for you. We'll see you there!

Administrator's Name/s
Date

FOLLOW-THROUGH

1. Assess the recognition's success.
2. Adjust your recognition plans, if needed.
3. Make up for a recognition event that did *not* go well. Do something else! It does not have to be expensive.
4. Remember a recognition event that *did* go well, and do it again!

When I was the principal of a middle school, my wonderful parents used to help me to appreciate the staff members by bringing food for them and placing it in the teachers' lounge. On Wednesdays, especially, they would bring muffins. Not mini-muffins or regu-

Wisdom Is the *Principal* Thing!

lar-sized muffins, but they would bring those huge muffins that had blueberries, chocolate chips, or macadamia nuts. They would do it *every* Wednesday like clockwork. Finally, I told them, "You guys are going to have to pick another day of the week to bring these muffins." "But why?" they asked. I said, "Because Wednesday is our church fast day, and you all are bringing these magnificent muffins, and I can't take the temptation anymore! What am I supposed to say? The devil made me do it?" They thought it was hilarious. This was my way of letting them know I noticed what they were doing and was grateful.

Find ways to let your staff, students, parents, and other volunteers know you appreciate them. It also would be very effective to learn *what* your school's constituents *prefer* in the way of appreciation and recognition. You can always do a survey at the beginning of the school year that includes ways they like to be appreciated. Sure, it takes time; however, personalizing recognition helps to increase morale, and it helps to solidify relationships.

A good head and a good heart are always a formidable combination.

Nelson Mandela

CHAPTER 20

SUPPORTING YOUR SUPERVISOR

It is the assistant's responsibility to support his or her supervisor. You are there to help your supervisor to lead an area of responsibility as effectively as possible. Two heads really are better than one, and your supervisor needs your ideas and expertise, whether it is stated or not. Actually, these tips can apply to any assistant's position, whether working in a school or in a department at the district level.

PREPARATION

Use Your Journalists' Questions!

1. **Who** is my supervisor (title/position)?
   Who am I to my supervisor? He or she could be at the elementary, middle or high school level, which will come with different expectations (title/position).
2. **What,** specifically, does my supervisor need from me (responsibilities)?
3. **When** does my supervisor need my support (times)?

Wisdom Is the *Principal* Thing!

4. **Where** does my supervisor need my support? **Where** does he or she need me to be (location)?
5. **Why** does my supervisor need my support (physical, mental, emotional, social; stand-in during absence; or for deadlines and requirements)?
6. **How** does my supervisor need me to support him or her (strategy)?

IMPLEMENTATION

Here Are Twelve Ways to Support Your Supervisor:

1. Be a catalyst and a problem-solver. Don't play the "I See-but-Don't-See Game." Be passionate about getting things done.

2. Be where you are needed *before* time, no less than on time, and be organized. Your supervisor needs to know that he or she can count on you to not only be there but also to have things in order. Believe it or not, your presence *before* things get started will be a load off of your supervisor's mind. Memorize your school or your department's calendar of events, so you can be proactive when it comes to planning, address-

Supporting Your Supervisor

ing, and resolving. If you know what is going on, and know what is to come, you can stay on top of things.

3. Don't *ever* go over his or her head, and don't go around him or her to get or do what you want. Do not complain to his or her boss. If you do take this risk, the word could get to the higher-ups that you cannot be trusted, and you could lessen your chances for a successful career.

4. Don't say "The-Boss-Made-Me-Do-It." It's a game that makes you the good guy and your supervisor, the bad guy. It undermines the supervisor and what he or she is endeavoring to accomplish. Say you are doing it for the good of the school, staff, and *all* students. Say you are following federal, state, and district guidelines.

5. Always, give a "heads up." Prepare your supervisor for everything that you can. Make sure he or she is aware. Do it aside and not in front of other people (staff, students, parents, or colleagues). If you allow your supervisor to be blindsided, it makes it appear that you are trying to convey that you are more on the ball than your boss.

Wisdom Is the *Principal* Thing!

6. Make sure you are always saying the same thing your supervisor is saying. Support his or her goals for the school or department. If you do not agree with the goals or feel you can't support them, you shouldn't be there.

7. Stay in your own lane! In other words, learn *your* duties and *do* them. Don't be so busy taking care of others' tasks that yours go lacking. If you do have a question about your boundaries, then ask your supervisor.

8. Involve people in decision-making. Involving staff members, students and parents in some decision-making will win them. People who are involved tend to be more supportive than those who aren't. Your supervisor will appreciate that your efforts have the support of others.

9. Do not change things without permission, especially, if they are a part of school procedures. If you disagree or have another idea, let your supervisor know. You do not have the authority to change a policy. You can make recommendations, but only your supervisor can make the changes. Your job is to enforce and support!

Supporting Your Supervisor

10. Don't be needy. You are there to assist, not to be assisted. Assistants in schools, in departments or to district leaders may say, "I need your support" when they really want the supervisors to do their jobs or make working easy. Back up and put that in reverse! Don't whine, complain, and make excuses. An assistant who takes high maintenance will not win the confidence of his or her boss.

11. Do your job well. Go above and beyond. This will not only be helpful to your supervisor, but it will also mold you into an excellent administrator and pave your way to moving up to the next level. Remember, mediocre assistants do not get promoted to a level where there are even *more* responsibilities.

12. Ask your supervisor if there are improvements that are needed in your performance *before* evaluation times. Continuous improvements in your performance will support her or him. This will be valued much more by your supervisor than if you wait to whine, complain and make excuses during and after evaluation times.

Wisdom Is the *Principal* Thing!

FOLLOW-THROUGH

Follow-through steps in this area take a certain kind of mentality. After you have implemented the steps toward a successful performance in your position, approach your tasks with the following in mind:

1. Be generous by asking your supervisor if there are ways that you can help, other than your regular duties.
2. Establish a healthy, working relationship with your supervisor. Let him or her know you personally care, not just professionally care.
3. Remember, your supervisor is *not* the enemy, no matter how overwhelmed or stressed out he, she, or you may get. It is the nature of the job.
4. Think of your supervisor as the leader of the team. You are all in it together, so you have to do what it takes to assist your supervisor in keeping the team together and completing the mission.
5. Remember also that things have a way of coming right back to you, so your support of your supervisor will result in you being supported by those *you* supervise. People watch what you do.

Supporting Your Supervisor

Implementing these steps has so much to do with having a great relationship with your supervisor and genuinely desiring success for him or her. It also shows you care about the school, department or district as a whole. Doing an outstanding job assisting your supervisor will ensure your chances for a successful career. People *will* take notice. Making your supervisor look good makes you look good too.

Synergize.

Stephen Covey

CHAPTER 21

TRAINING COORDINATION

Keep a list of qualified contacts for different kinds of trainings. If the budget allows for it, bringing people from the outside to train your staff can be great; however, this can get complicated, pending availability.

Sometimes, a new or fresh face is needed to boost morale or peak interest; however, consider giving opportunities to qualified people *already* on your staff. This will not only help them to grow, but it will also let them know how much you value them and appreciate their willingness to share their expertise with their colleagues.

Using the journalists' questions, much of the information concerning in-school trainings may be applied to the typical parent and community, whole staff, department, or team meetings.

IN-SCHOOL TRAININGS

PREPARATION

Use Your Journalists' Questions!

Wisdom Is the *Principal* Thing!

1. **Who** will be *invited* to come to the training?
   Who will be *required* to come to the training?
   Who has the *expertise* to conduct the training?

2. **What** will be the content of the training?
   What information needs to be compiled if you are conducting it?

3. **When** will it be conducted?
   - Date
   - Time

   When will it begin and when will it end?
   - Half day
   - One to two hours
   - Two or more days
   - Whole day

4. **Where** at the school will it be held?
   - Auditorium
   - Cafeteria
   - Classroom
   - Media Center
   - Multipurpose room
   - Outside (teamwork activities, etc.)

   Where at another location will it be held?
   - Another local school
   - A local district facility

Training Coordination

- A local community facility
- On local community grounds

Where specifically will it be held? Provide the address, including

- ➢ Building and floor number
- ➢ Room or suite number
- ➢ Street number

5. **Why** is the training being conducted?
   - ➢ Goal
   - ➢ Purpose

   Why is the district, state, or federal government requiring it?

   Why do your staff members need it?
   - ➢ Licensure/Certification
   - ➢ Strategies to enhance effectiveness (including updated techniques)

6. **How** will the training be structured?
   How will participants be involved?
   - ➢ Group work
   - ➢ Lectures
   - ➢ Moving around
   - ➢ Podcasts or webinars
   - ➢ Sitting down

   How will the following occur?
   - ➢ Presenters recruited

Wisdom Is the *Principal* Thing!

- Using in-house resources
- Using outside resources
- Presenters compensated
  - Gifts
  - Stipend/budget fees
- Food purchased
- Notification of those you are *requiring* to attend
- Notification of those you are *inviting* to attend
- Use of learned information
  - In classroom
  - Train-the-trainer sessions (Those trained to train others)

IMPLEMENTATION

1. Be knowledgeable of the types of out-of-school trainings that are available for sending your staff members.
   - District required
   - Federally required or recommended
   - School required
   - State required
   - Others are as follows:
     - Attendance

Training Coordination

- Curricular techniques in content areas
- Discipline
- Diverse/cultural teaching strategies
- Leadership and administration
- Motivation
- New teachers
- Programs and projects
- Parent communication
- Safety and security
- Teamwork
- Technology
- Testing

2. Decide how the training should be structured to maximize effectiveness, according to the needs and requirements for your school. Get input from some of those who will be involved in the training.
3. Try to confirm attendance numbers as much as possible. You will need to have the number of people you expect to attend, in order to plan for the following, so decide how many of these things you need:
    - Handouts and other materials
    - Props or field equipment pieces

Wisdom Is the *Principal* Thing!

- ➢ LCD, projector, screen, computer accessibility, PowerPoint capabilities
- ➢ Tables and seats
- ➢ Light refreshments, full or continental breakfast items, or full or light lunch items

4. Arrive at the location early to set up the area where the training will occur. Ask others to help you, if possible.
5. Make sure the technology is working *before* the training begins! Test the logistics too.
6. Have someone designated to give handouts to the participants, so they will not have to wait while the presenter does it.
7. Always have a sign-in sheet for the records. Make certain the sign-in sheet requests the pertinent information needed to submit for credits. Remind the participants at the beginning and end to sign the sheet. This will eliminate "discussions" when it comes time for proof for credit renewals and licensure requirements.
8. Give housekeeping instructions at the beginning of the trainings, so the participants will know what is acceptable for taking restroom breaks and snack breaks.
9. Tell the purpose and benefits of the training for the participants.

Training Coordination

10. Give reasonable time for breaks. Train in sections, and don't give too much information at one time. You will want people to remember what is being presented.
11. Make sure there is ample time for questions and other interactions.
12. Tell what is expected of the participants, once the training is completed. Will they be expected to use the information to train others (train-the trainer) or just use it themselves to be more effective in their positions?
13. If a train-the-trainer model is to be used, explain how it will be structured, or tell the participants when they can expect to be informed about future requirements.

It's always good to have a Plan "B"! Be prepared to use old fashioned methods, if necessary, to present. Even if a place where I am presenting has a computer, I take my laptop and projector anyway, just in case. Once, I was conducting a workshop at an elementary school. The power cut off unexpectedly, and I was not able to use the technology I had planned to use. The principal asked me to continue with the presentation, even though it was semi-dark in the library where we were. I had to resort to standing by a window to use the light from outside and present-

Wisdom Is the *Principal* Thing!

ing from the handouts that I had prepared, thank goodness! It is a good idea to always have handouts with the major points of the training, so the participants can follow your presentation, whether you have technology plans or not.

OUT-OF-SCHOOL TRAININGS

PREPARATION

There will be trainings where you will need to or will wish to send some of your staff members. These may be regional, district, state or national trainings.

Use Your Journalists' Questions!

1. **Who** will be *invited* to attend the training?
   Who will be *required* to attend the training?
   Who has the *expertise* to conduct the training?

2. **What** will be the content of the training? What will your staff members need to learn?
   What information must be compiled for your staff members to go?
   - Mileage forms
   - Registration forms
   - Request forms

Training Coordination

What resources must be obtained for your staff members to attend?
- ➤ Accommodations
  - Hotels reservations
  - Family or friends' homes
- ➤ Materials
  - Books/Packets
  - Technological resources
- ➤ Transportation modes
  - Flights
  - Buses or trains
  - Vehicles
    - ✓ Rental
    - ✓ Personal with reimbursed mileage

3. **When** will it be conducted?
   - ➤ Date
   - ➤ Time

   When will it begin and when will it end?
   - ➤ Half day
   - ➤ One to two hours
   - ➤ Two or more days
   - ➤ Whole day

4. **Where** at another location will it be held?

Wisdom Is the *Principal* Thing!

- ➢ Another local school
- ➢ A school district facility
- ➢ A community facility
- ➢ Another city location
- ➢ Another state location
- ➢ International location

Where specifically will it be held? Provide the address, including
- ➢ Building and floor number
- ➢ Country, state, city
- ➢ Room or suite number
- ➢ Street number

5. **Why** is the training being conducted?
    - ➢ Goal
    - ➢ Purpose

    Why is the state or school district requiring it?
    Why do your school staff members need it?
    - ➢ Licensure/Certification
    - ➢ Strategies for more effectiveness (including updated techniques)

6. **How** will the training be structured?
    How will participants be involved?
    - ➢ Group work
    - ➢ Lectures
    - ➢ Moving around

Training Coordination

- Podcasts or Webinars
- Sitting down

How will the following occur?

- Resources attained
  - Allotments for professional development
    - ✓ District budget
    - ✓ School budget
    - ✓ State budget
  - Federal grants
  - International grants
- Notification of those you are *requiring* to attend
- Notification of those you are *inviting* to attend
- Response to the requests from staff members to attend – Maintain equity.
  - Administrative decision
  - Committee decision
  - Licensure/Certification
  - First come, first served
  - Need for training
  - Staff seniority
- Use of information in the classroom and in the train-the-trainer sessions

Wisdom Is the *Principal* Thing!

IMPLEMENTATION

1. Be knowledgeable of the types of out-of-school trainings that are available for sending your staff members.
    - District or state required
    - Federally required or recommended
    - Internationally recommended
    - Others are as follows:
        - Attendance
        - Culturally diverse instructional practices
        - Cutting edge instructional techniques
        - Data driven instructional strategies
        - Discipline
        - Leadership/Administration
        - New teachers
        - Parent communication
        - Programs and projects
        - Online teaching
        - Safety and security
        - Teamwork
        - Technology
        - Testing

Training Coordination

2. Decide how the training will help maximize the effectiveness of your staff members. Get input from other leaders of teams and departments at your school. Confirm attendance numbers as soon as possible to calculate fees.
   - Registration fees
   - Flight tickets
   - Vans, cars or buses
   - Mileage logs as well as food reimbursement forms
   - Number of hotel rooms
3. Find out the exact locations for hotels and training sessions.
4. Find out what materials or technology they will need. Do they need to take laptops or tablets?
5. Remind the participants to bring proof of their attendance and participation in all of the sessions required. This will eliminate "discussions" concerning proof for credit renewals/licensure requirements. Hence, this will also help to deter shenanigans and elevate motives while they are away.
6. Make sure the participants know the purpose of the training, how the training will benefit them, and how the training will benefit their students.
7. Decide if the participants will be expected to use the new knowledge to train others or just

Wisdom Is the *Principal* Thing!

   use the information themselves to be more effective in their positions?
8. If a train-the-trainer model is to be used, tell the participants *when* they will be informed about the expectations.

Your school's budget will determine how often you will be able to send teachers to trainings that are not funded by your district or state. Try to reserve a portion of your professional development budget for *some* outside trainings without negatively impacting another area. You will be thrilled how much a new perspective can impact, motivate, and refocus your staff members.

FOLLOW-THROUGH

1. Give the newly trained participants the expectations for using the information they learned in the classroom.
2. Give the train-the-trainer personnel, who are expected to train the other staff members, the schedule and structure of the model.
3. Give the train-the-trainer personnel the time to plan their training sessions.
4. Give incentives for those who train others and give incentives to trainees such as certificates.

Training Coordination

5. Make sure there is a budget for the train-the-trainer model sessions.
6. Try to confirm attendance numbers at the train-the-trainer sessions as much as possible as you prepare for the following:
    - Handouts and other materials
    - Props or field equipment pieces
    - Projector/LCD, screen, PowerPoint capabilities, computer accessibility, light refreshments, full or continental breakfast items, and full or light lunch items
    - Tables and seats

Obviously, the world is moving toward more online trainings; however, whether an in-school, out-of-school, or online training, a new excitement about teaching and learning can be infectious in a positive way! It can be a shot in the arm and can boost the morale among your staff members! Provide these opportunities as much as possible.

Leadership and learning are indispensable to each other.

President John F. Kennedy

CHAPTER 22

TWELVE TIPS FOR THE WISE

1. **Get to know your staff members right away.**
   a. **Memorize the names and faces of the staff members before your first day on the job.** When I received my first assignment as an assistant principal, the principal of the school had a staff gathering at her home to introduce the staff members to the two new assistant principals, and I was one of them. Before the party, I went to the school and requested the previous years' yearbook. I memorized the pictures and names of the entire staff. I was able to greet almost all of them by name before they could tell me who they were. They were impressed. I came off as a "go-getter" from the beginning! Even more important, I knew the staff members' names. That was very helpful in my new position!
   b. **Get to know the staff members well that are in key positions,** *offi-*

cially. These include the cafeteria manager, head custodian, curriculum facilitators, counselors, secretaries, school nurse, school psychologist, school social worker, school resource officer, coaches, Media Center specialists, team leaders, chairpersons of departments, and other administrators.

    c. **Get to know the staff members well that are in key positions, *unofficially*.** You know what I mean. Ms. Smart who has been teaching at the school for fifteen years and everybody looks up to her? Get to know her and <u>win</u> her! Build strong, positive relationships, which will be the key to the success of all of your interactions with others.

2. **Know your school's mission statement and your school's goals.** Keep repeating them to yourself like a mantra. This will help you to focus and not become apathetic or become complacent in your position. Be passionate about the mission. Terminate all negative thoughts and feelings, whether

they arise within you or come from someone else. Find the positive aspects of your job and keep striving to become even better at what you do. Be like a breath of fresh air. You will love yourself, and others will love you too.

3. **Get to know the administrative colleagues at your school and at other schools.** Feel free to call someone and *be generous* when someone calls you to see how to address an issue or to implement something. Don't be a loner. Be friendly and helpful, and you will receive the same response when you need help. It's not weak. Being a "Know-it-all" makes you weak, especially when a colleague has experienced what you are going through and can give you some wise advice.

4. **Set up email, text, GroupMe, Zoom and other groups.** Take the time to set up these groups before the teachers and students arrive for their first day of the school year. For example, typical email or other types of groups for an assistant principal may be grade level teachers, counselors, depart-

Wisdom Is the *Principal* Thing!

ment chairpersons, curriculum facilitators (literacy, math, and technical), teacher assistants, team leaders, elective teachers, coaches, after-school staff members, and leaders of parent groups.

5. **Dress to impress!** People in the business world dress more casual these days, but always dress *professionally*. There will be dress-down days, and yes, you should participate to show you are a member of the team. Parents, students, and teachers form opinions about administrators, depending upon the way they dress. They should be able to look at you and know you are the professional. If you don't feel that great when you get up one morning, dress even better than usual. By the time everyone tells you how wonderful you look, you'll *feel* better!

6. **Do not hang with clicks or show favoritism**. It will backfire. When I say, "clicks," I mean unofficial and social groups.
    a. First, unofficial groups are not school designated teams, grade levels or departments. These are groups that have

Twelve Tips for the Wise

formed at the school and meet during free times and/or groups that have formed to enjoy time together outside of the school. There is nothing wrong with comradery and companionship. There is something *very* wrong when groups form and say or do things that negatively impact or cause dissention within school operations or within the school's program as a whole.

b. Second, unofficial groups or clicks may invite you to join their discussions and activities such as Friday nights at a restaurant. They may ask you questions, supposedly, "off the record." As an administrator, you must be *whole-school and total-staff minded* at all times, even when you are off campus. To be seen as part of a certain group or click will cause division and distrust from the others who are not a part of it. It is your responsibility to encourage and support all of the official groups that are a part of your school. Everyone *must* know that you will do just as much to support one group as you will to support another.

Wisdom Is the *Principal* Thing!

Remember, "Nothing is ever 'off the record.' You will hear it again."

7. **Remain professional, even on *social media*.** It's fine to have a great time, post some great photos, and generate some laughs. However, remember that parents, students, your bosses and the community will form opinions about your character by the things they see, hear, and read that involve you. Some of you may not agree, but I encourage you to think twice before using profanity or vulgarity, making sexual innuendos, or acting unseemly at work or on social media. I know it's your business, but you don't *ever* want your character to come into question because of something you said at work or posted on Facebook, Twitter or Instagram, do you? Just remember who and what you represent. You still represent your workplace, even when you are *not* there!

8. **Be just as respectful of non-certified staff members as you are of certified staff members.** Address them by their titles (Mr. Ms.) and last names, especially in

Twelve Tips for the Wise

front of students. It is not professional and very humiliating for a student to call a staff member by the first name. I once heard a student call the head custodian by his first name and tell him he needed to clean something up. This is unacceptable, and I let that student know it.

9. **Delegate or Die**. "DD"! The principals in Charlotte-Mecklenburg Schools used this acronym very often. When they said it, they meant you must find a way to delegate some of your duties, or you will not last. There are willing staff members, parents and volunteers. At one of my schools, one of the duties that was assigned to me when I took the position was to keep the school marquee updated. The marquee was on the side of the school building, several feet above the ground, and could only be accessed with a *ladder*! The previous assistant principal would climb the ladder and place the magnetic letters to keep announcements current. Well, I was twenty years older than she was, and I was not going to climb any ladders. So, one of the teachers happened to visit me in my of-

Wisdom Is the *Principal* Thing!

fice, and I talked with him about this duty. This teacher *offered* to update and maintain the marquee with the help of his homeroom students. All I had to do was email the new announcements to him, and he and his students would plan the lettering. They would hand them to him as he climbed the ladder and updated the announcements. He and his students did this for me the entire time that I worked at the school. It saved me so much time! Don't allow yourself to become burned out and become a walking zombie on the job. We have too much of that already. Find a way to get teachers and parents to help you. If you develop a positive relationship with them, they will even *offer* to help you. Remember! **D**elegate or **D**ie!

10. **Read, when you have time.** Read for pleasure to take mini-sabbaticals and read for self-help. You can either read a book, or you can download reading material on your phone, tablet or computer. You will be surprised at the insightful information you can pull from reading that may give

Twelve Tips for the Wise

you confidence, give you hope, and help you to be more effective in your position.

11. **Remember and use The Three *T*'s.** My father often talked with me about tact. My mother often talked with me about timing. Frequently, my husband talked with me about tone. No matter the issue or situation, using tactfulness, choosing the right time, and choosing the appropriate tone makes all of the difference in **how** *what you have to say* is received. In all communications, always remember **The Three *T*'s: Tact, Timing, and Tone.**

12. **Find the humor.** Humor has a way of easing the tension that can come from being a supervisor. You, supervisors, have to discipline, teach, hire, fire, address complaints, address successes, address failures, keep bosses and employees satisfied, and much more. Finding the humor in everyday situations can help you to maintain a healthy perspective, so your mentality and views won't become askew or extreme. Humor brings balance. In your everyday dealings with all types of people from all

Wisdom Is the *Principal* Thing!

walks of life, find the humor. Even Dwight D. Eisenhower said, "In that lifelong pursuit [of happiness] a sense of humor can relieve tension, soothe the pain of disappointment and strengthen the spirit for the formidable tasks that always lie ahead" (1958). So, find the right time, and when you are by yourself or with the right people, go ahead and chuckle, laugh, roar! Whatever the situation, reflect on it with a merry heart. It will relieve your stress too!

Put first things first.

Stephen Covey

FINAL THOUGHTS

Use the simple strategy of applying the journalists' questions to any task; Use preparation, implementation and follow-through as a three-pronged approach to every project; Use organizing and delegating effectively every day; and use The Three *T*'s in all communications, which will help you to form lasting relationships. These patterns run through this book and are necessary for *favorable results,* wherever you are and whatever your situation.

I attribute much of my success to the wisdom of developing positive relationships with my students, parents, staff members, colleagues, supervisors, and community members as I carried out my daily duties.

Relationships! Relationships! Relationships! I cannot say it enough. Positive relationships are critical. They build bridges. They tear down barriers. They forge bonds that will make your work much easier, and they will pave your way to success.

Hence, wisdom is the *principal* thing. Use it!

END NOTES

Buehner, Carl W. Quoted in *Richard Evans' Quote Book* by Richard L. Evans, p. 244, Copyright 1971. Extract used by permission by Atesons Publishers.

Covey, Stephen, R. (1981), *Principle-Centered Leadership*. New York: Simon & Schuster. 1981. Print. Extracts from Chapter 2 Pages 40 – 47 and Chapter 24, page 249 used with permission by the Franklin Covey Co.

Eisenhower, Dwight D. (1957, November 14) "Remarks at the National Defense Executive Reserve Conference." Online by Gerhard Peters and John T. Woolley, *The American Presidency Project. Retrieved from* http//ww.presidency.uscb.edu/ws/?pid=10951.

Eisenhower, Dwight D. (1958, June 4). "Address at U.S. Naval Academy Commencement." Online by Gerhard Peters and John T. Woolley.
The American Presidency Project. Retrieved from
http//ww.presidency.uscb.edu/ws/?pid=11080.

Eisenhower, Dwight D. (1954, April 29) "Remarks to the leaders of the United Defense Fund." Online by Dwight D. Eisenhower Presidential Library, Museum

Wisdom Is the *Principal* Thing!

and Boyhood Home. Abilene, Kansas. Presidential Libraries System. *Quotes*: "Leadership/Organization."

Half, Robert. (2017, March 1) "World's Most Admired Companies." *Fortune Magazine*. 1 March 2017. Web. Retrieved May 18, 2017.
https://www.roberthalf.com/blog/10-awesome-career-quotes-that-will-inspire-and-motivate-you.

Hall, Trent P. (2012, March 25) "Kathy and King's Quote." Photographed. 9:05 AM. JPEG file.

Hammond, Thaddeus (1925, September). quoted in J. R. Sprague's "Big Business-itis, *"The Rotarian"* Vol. XXVII, No 3, p. 6.

Hunter, Madeline *Madeline Hunter's Mastery Teaching*: Increasing Instructional Effectiveness in Elementary and Secondary Schools, Colleges and Universities. (1982, June) Tip Pubns. Print. Extracts used with permission of the Copyright Clearance Center.

Jay, John, (1893). The Correspondence and Public Papers of John Jay, ed. Henry P. Johnston. Letter to Rev. Dr. Jedediah Morse (1813 Bedford). New York: G.P. Putnams's Sons, Vol 4 (1794-1826).

End Notes

Johnson, Harold K. Gen. (1985) Department of the Army Pamphlet 600—65. Leadership Statements and Quotes. p. 18. Headquarters: Department of the Army. Washington, DC. Used with permission by United States Army.

Kennedy, John F. (1963, November 22) Intended for remarks at the Dallas Trade Mart. Retrieved from http://www.presidency.ucsb.edu/ws/index.php?pid=9539&st=Trade+Mart&st1=).

King, Martin Luther, Jr. (1947) "The Purpose of Education." Student Paper. *The Maroon Tiger*. Atlanta: Morehouse College.

Maslow, Abraham. (1943). "A Theory of Human Motivation." Paper by Abraham Maslow.
Psychological Review #50 1943. Reference used with permission from Maslow@Maslow.com.

Meer, Fatima. (1990). *The Authorized Nelson Mandela: Higher Than Hope*. New York: Harper & Row. Letter to Fatima Meer, written on Robben Island. Jan 1, 1976. Extract used with permission from the Nelson Mandela Foundation.

Plato. Public Domain

Wisdom Is the *Principal* Thing!

Roosevelt, Theodore. (1913). *Theodore Roosevelt: An Autobiography*. New York: Charles Scribner's Sons. Quoted Bill Widener. Chapter IX, page 327.

"Wisdom is the principal thing: Therefore get wisdom: and with all thy getting, get understanding."
Proverbs 4:7 from the Authorized Version of the Bible (King James Bible). "Extracts from the Authorized Version of the Bible (The King James Bible), the rights in which are vested in the Crown, are reproduced by permission of the Crown's Patentee, Cambridge University Press."

Ziglar, Zig. Used with permission by the Zig Ziglar Corporation. www.Ziglar.com.

Note: Most citations are written as specified by the copyright holders.
Also, *GCABSE* is an acronym for the Greater Charlotte Alliance of Black School Educators, which is an affiliate of the National Alliance of Black School Educators (*NABSE*).

APPENDICES

During your administrative tenure, there will be many reasons for you to send written communication to someone. Written communications can be in many forms: Letters, memos, emails, website and social media posts, and sections of school newsletters and bulletins. Letters may become any of the other forms, as long as the correct format is used. Although lengths and styles may vary, all written communications should include specific elements, so there will be no confusion concerning the sender's intent and expectations.

Use Your Journalists' Questions!

1. **Who** is addressed in the written communication?
    - Community personnel
    - District or state personnel
    - Parent
    - Supervisor
    - Teacher or another staff member

2. **What** is the content of the letter?
    - Award, recognition, and/or achievement

Wisdom Is the *Principal* Thing!

- Information or awareness
- Opening of school procedures
- PTA/PTO Event
- Response or confirmation
- Student, teacher or parent concern

What is the style of the information?
- Business letter format
- Memo format
- Email format
- School newsletter
- Website announcement

3. **When** will things in the letter occur?
   When did things in the letter occur?
   - Dates?
   - Times?

4. **Where** will things in the letter occur?
   Where did things in the letter occur?
   - Address of school
   - Location within school
     - Classroom
     - Conference room
     - Media Center
     - Multi-Purpose Room
     - Office
   - Address of district or state building

Appendices

- ➢ Location within district or state building
  - Conference room
  - Floor
  - Office
  - Suite

5. **Why** do you need to write and send this letter? The purpose?
   - ➢ Confirm follow-up plans
   - ➢ Make an assignment
   - ➢ Make or accept an invitation
   - ➢ Make a request
   - ➢ Reminder of action items
   - ➢ Require something
   - ➢ Say "Thank you"
   - ➢ Submit information
   - ➢ Summarize a conference or meeting

6. **How** will action items in the letter be addressed?
   - ➢ How will things be structured?
   - ➢ How will things be resolved?

Once you have answered all of your journalists' questions, it will be easy for you to apply the answers to the following *eight key elements* that should be included in every written communication:

Wisdom Is the *Principal* Thing!

The Eight Elements of Written Communication:

1. Receiver's name and contact information
2. Purpose of the written communication
   - Subject
   - Issue
   - Concerns
3. Dates, times and locations
4. Recommendations and resolutions
5. Future expectations of participants
6. Sender's title/position and contact information
7. List of enclosures
8. Names of others who are receiving a copy (cc)

Here are a few samples that you may use by inserting your own information in the parts that are underlined. Fictional names and titles are used in all templates.

The following letters may be freely used, provided you have purchased this book. They may be scanned into a compatible document file that you may revise as needed with the names, the dates, and the specific details of your situations. They can be sent as letters, memos, or emails.

Appendices

The observation form elements can be copied or downloaded and can be easily cut and pasted to make a practical observation form for immediate use.

Appendices

A: Follow-Up Letter for Assignment to a Discipline School

Date

Muffet Cottontail
5000 Winterland Lane
Fairytale, NC 55555

Re: Your Child, Peter Cottontail

Dear Mrs. Cottontail,

The purpose of this letter is to inform you that Peter has been assigned to Briar Patch High School, beginning Monday, Date. Please have him at Briar Patch School for an intake conference at Time on Date. A packet and an informational booklet are attached to this letter. Please take the packet and informational booklet to the intake conference with you also. The packet includes his discipline record and information regarding an event which occurred on Date. Peter was referred for assaulting another male student and by showing disrespect to his teacher when the teacher tried to address the behavior. Peter has 24 discipline offenses on his discipline

Wisdom Is the *Principal* Thing!

record, which include 16 times in In-school Suspensions and 3 Out-of-school suspensions.

Please give me a call or email me and let me know that you received this packet and also if you have any questions concerning the incident that occurred today. You may call Briar Patch School at Number if you have questions about their procedures that may need to be clarified after reading the Briar Patch School booklet.

It is my desire that Peter have a successful experience at Briar Patch that will enable him to return with a new and positive approach to his school life here at Bunny Trail School.

Sincerely,

Your Name
Your Title
1-BUN-NYT-RAIL
HappyTime@bunnytrailschool.edu

cc: Your Immediate Supervisor

Appendices

B: Letter for Notification of an Expulsion

Date

George Contrary
5000 Silver Bells Lane
Fairytale, NC 55555

Re: Your Child, Mary Contrary

Dear Mr. Contrary:

On Date, your child, Mary Contrary, engaged in the following behavior:
Mary walked in and began screaming at a student in Ms. Garden's class. Ms. Garden was holding detention for other students and reported that there was no reason for Mary to be in her room because she did not have detention with Ms. Garden that period. Ms. Garden told Mary to leave her room. Mary left and walked down the hall toward Ms. Rowhill's room. Ms. Rowhill reported that Mary was seen cursing, screaming, and using profanity such as "---- you" and "Go to h---" at *another* student. Ms. Rowhill reported that a fight was in the making, with other students beginning to form a crowd. When Ms. Rowhill tried to guide Mary away so there wouldn't

Wisdom Is the *Principal* Thing!

<u>be a fight, Mary began screaming at Ms. Rowhill, "Don't touch me! Take your "D----- hands off me!" and assaulted her by punching her in the stomach. The principal suspended Mary, pending a hearing, considering her previous 10 violations this semester.</u>

Therefore, I, <u>Your Name</u>, under the direction of the principal, have acted to suspend <u>Mary</u> from school immediately and have recommended that a Hearing Officer determine if expulsion from school is appropriate.

A hearing in this matter has been scheduled for <u>Time</u>, on <u>Date</u>. The hearing will take place at <u>Name of Place, and Address with</u> <u>Building/Suite/Floor</u>. If you need directions, please call <u>Number of School.</u> You and <u>Mary</u>, are <u>required</u> to attend and participate in this hearing.

<u>Mary</u> will not be permitted to return to school until you have completed the hearing process and a decision is made. Persons to be present for the hearing are an administrator, you as the parent or guardian, <u>Mary</u>, and the hearing officer. If you plan to attend with legal counsel, please notify me in writing immediately so that arrangements can be made for the

Appendices

district's legal counsel to attend. Failure to do so may cause the hearing to be rescheduled.
Please feel free to call the school or email me with any questions you might have.

Sincerely,

Your Name,
Your Title
1-BUN-NYT-RAIL
HappyTime@bunnytrailschool.edu

cc: Your Immediate Supervisor

Wisdom Is the *Principal* Thing!

C: Letter for Teacher Recognition

Date

Lucy Locket
1111 Bunnytrail School
Fairytale, NC 55555

Dear Miss Locket,

I want to take the time to congratulate you on your recent recognition as the 2018 – 2019 Teacher of the Year for North Carolina. I have personally observed your continuous dedication to the education of all children, and your award is well deserved. Not only have you been instrumental in helping to incorporate cultural awareness in teaching techniques, but you also have gone above and beyond expectations, time and time again, to help us to accomplish all elements of our school's vision. The parents, students, community, and district personnel appreciate how you unselfishly give your time and skills to the cause.

Please know that you are greatly appreciated, and I join all others who applaud you and your accomplishments. It is my desire that you receive all of the

Appendices

accolades you are due as you continue to be a positive force in children's lives.

Sincerely,

Your Name,
Your Title
1-BUN-NYT-RAIL
HappyTime@bunnytrailschool.edu

cc. Your immediate supervisor

Wisdom Is the *Principal* Thing!

D: Letter to Parents for a Student's Accomplishment

Date

Jack and Cindy Greenway
2222 Primrose Lane
Fairytale, NC 55555

Dear Mr. and Mrs. Greenway,

I want to take the time to congratulate you and your son, Handsome Greenway, on his recent recognition as Most Outstanding Student for the Nursery Rhyme School District for the year 2018-2019. Handsome's award is well deserved as I have personally observed his continual commitment to the preservation of the environment. Not only has he been instrumental in aiding us in implementing our school goals for environmental protection and beauty, but he also has gone above and beyond expectations to cheerfully help accomplish these goals for our district. He has proven to be an awesome role model for other students who have also enthusiastically joined the project.

The parents, students, community and district appreciate how he has unselfishly given his time and skills

Appendices

to <u>this project</u>. Please know that <u>Handsome</u> is greatly appreciated, and I join all others who applaud you as the parents of one who has such outstanding accomplishments. It is my desire that he receives all of the recognitions he is due as you continue to be a supportive force in his life, and he continues to be an encouraging force in the lives of others.

<u>Your Name</u>,
Your Title
<u>1-BUN-NYT-RAIL</u>
<u>HappyTime@bunnytrailschool.edu</u>

cc: <u>Your immediate supervisor</u>

Wisdom Is the *Principal* Thing!

E: Letter to Request a Conference

<u>Date</u>

<u>Ms. Sunny Day</u>
<u>1111 Bunnytrail School</u>
<u>Fairytail, NC 55555</u>

Dear Ms. Day,

The purpose of this letter is to set a conference with <u>you, your team members, and me</u> to be held on <u>date</u> in <u>my office</u>. I am requesting this conference because <u>it was brought to my attention that there are some concerns about the team dynamics and effectiveness concerning decision-making about the best paths to take to educate *all* of your students.</u> Each of your teammates have received this same <u>memo/letter</u>. Please inform me, immediately, if <u>there is any reason you cannot meet at the beginning of your planning period on the above noted date.</u> Bring any documentation you feel will <u>be helpful in aiding and fostering a resolution to these concerns.</u>

I am asking each of you to reflect on <u>the priorities</u> and come to the meeting <u>with an open mind</u>. It is my desire that this meeting will result in strategies that

Appendices

will aid you as team members to not only be effective in teaching but also enhance the learning of all of your students. This is our purpose. Come with our school's theme in mind: <u>Enhance Learning for All Students with the Best of Our Abilities and Resources</u>. I will see all of you on <u>date</u>.

<u>Your Name</u>,
<u>Your Title</u>
<u>1-BUN-NYT-RAIL</u>
<u>HappyTime@bunnytrailschool.edu</u>

cc. <u>Team Members</u>
   <u>Your Immediate Supervisor</u>

Wisdom Is the *Principal* Thing!

F: Letter to Teacher Summarizing a Conference

<u>Date</u>

<u>Georgie Porgie</u>
<u>1111 Bunnytrail School</u>
<u>Fairytail, NC 55555</u>

Dear Mr. Porgie,

The purpose of this letter is to summarize the conference held on <u>date</u> in <u>my office</u>. The conference was held because <u>three female teachers</u> here at <u>Bunnytrail School have complained that you have made inappropriate comments to them</u>. Per our discussion, the following are the requirements you must meet so that <u>no further complaints of this nature are received</u>:

1. Since you indicated in the conference that <u>you are having trouble distinguishing what is appropriate or not, restrict your conversations to school issues only.</u>
2. Talk to <u>these teachers only when your job requires you to do so and keep the interaction short and to the point.</u>
3. Do not comment upon or refer to <u>any female teacher's appearance or actions.</u>

Appendices

4. If at any point, <u>a teacher lets you know she is uncomfortable with something you have stated, end the conversation immediately, put your school related business (only what you are required to communicate) in writing, and send it to her.</u>
5. If you think <u>a teacher is interested in having more than a business relationship with you, she must give you her personal information, and you can only meet with her for personal reasons after school and away from the school campus.</u>
6. If anyone <u>makes *you* feel uncomfortable, inform me immediately.</u>

If any further complaints are made after your receipt of this letter, you will be referred to Human Resources for a formal process to begin, according to district and state regulations. It is my desire that you learn to use wisdom in <u>your communications with other staff members</u>. They are your colleagues, and <u>nothing you say or do should ever bring this kind of discomfort.</u>

Sincerely,

<u>Your Name,</u>

Wisdom Is the *Principal* Thing!

Your Title
1-BUN-NYT-RAIL
HappyTime@bunnytrailschool.edu

cc: Your Immediate Supervisor

Appendices

G: Teacher Observation Form

Teacher: Subject Area: Observer:
Date: Time: Objective/Concept:

Objective Appropriate? Yes/No

Preparation:
— Has accurate and up-to-date lesson plans
— Has lesson plans compatible to school and district goals
— Has materials prepared and available
— Has designed information that is sequential and organized to see the relationships of the parts to the whole
— Has given students the resources they need

Instructional Presentation
— Gets students' attention and engages them quickly
— Introduces the concept and reinforces importance
— Models and gives examples
— Gives guided practices
— Uses appropriate pace, and transitions are efficient and smooth
— Summarizes the concepts taught
— Assigns independent practice to reinforce learning

Wisdom Is the *Principal* Thing!

Facilitating and Enhancing Learning
— Uses varied instructional methods, appropriate for student abilities, rates, and learning styles
— Engages students actively in learning
— Promotes critical thinking, problem solving, and collaborative learning
— Maintains and reinforces appropriate expectations for students' abilities
— Uses technology to enhance learning
— Uses oral, written, and other work products to enhance learning

Instructional Monitoring and Assessment
— Uses appropriate questioning techniques
— Uses effective instructional feedback
— Uses informal assessment strategies
— Circulates to check all students' performances and evaluates all ability levels
— Uses formal assessment integrated for complexity and length of unit

Managing Student Behavior
— Establishes rules that are clear and appropriate
— Establishes rules that govern verbal participation and movement during transitions, whole-class, small group, and seat-work activities
— Enforces rules fairly and consistently

Appendices

Managing the Learning Environment
— Manages materials, resources and technologies
— Maintains accurate student records
— Treats all students in a fair and equitable manner
— Produces a welcoming physical environment
— Uses clear and accurate written language
— Promotes positive student to student and teacher to teacher interactions

Comments:

_____
Observer Signature

Appendices

H: Find the Humor!

Here are a few situations where I just found the humor. Even when I recounted them to other people, they would chuckle too.

1. Having previously worked for a very large school district, I knew I was working for a small school district when, as the newly hired assistant principal, I asked the secretary for a list of courier numbers for the schools and departments. She politely said, "Oh, Honey, just put the person's name and their school or department on it and put it in the Pony!" "The Pony?" I asked. "Yeah, like the Pony Express?" was the clarification. I just shook my head and chuckled all of the way to the Pony!

2. I was having a conference with a parent about her child's behavior and all of a sudden, the lady jumped up from her chair, and shouted, "You go to hell!" She went out and slammed the door to my office so hard that the ceiling tiles cracked and some of the pieces fell on my head. Ceiling tiles and that chalky stuff were all over my desk, on my clothes, and in my hair. Other

Wisdom Is the *Principal* Thing!

staff members, including my principal, heard the noise and ran to my office to see what had happened. After recounting the incident, including where she told me to go, I concluded with "…but, I don't think I'll go to hell today. I'm going to my hairdresser!"

3. I was in my office when I received a call on the radio that a student was on her way to my office with a referral from a classroom teacher. The student walked in, tossed the discipline referral on my desk, and sat down in a chair. With her arms folded, her legs crossed, and her face turned to the side, she refused to look at me, and her body language was one of pure defiance. I studied her for a moment. She had black fingernail polish and toenail polish, black lipstick, black eyeliner that was heavily applied, and black hair. She was dressed in a black T-shirt, black jeans, black shoes, and she had little silver rings on each finger. *The gothic look*, I guessed. *Okay, no problem*, I thought. "Let's see what we have here." I read the referral which stated that she had been disrespect-

Appendices

ful to the teacher by talking back to her and throwing her paper down. When I looked up at her, she had turned toward me to study my expression as I read the referral. I then noticed the statement on her T-shirt. "Blame it on my mother," it said.

4. **Student**: Ms. Hall, my teacher told me I have to go to *Saturday* School!
   Ms. Hall: Okay, you look a little confused about it. What's wrong?
   Student: Why do I have to go to Saturday School? I came to school all week!
   Ms. Hall: Well, if you are assigned to Saturday School, that means there are some things that you have not been learning during the week, and we hope you will learn more and understand better on Saturdays.
   Student: Okay, so do I still have to come during the week?
   Ms. Hall: Yes, you do.
   Student: Why, when you and the teacher think I can learn *more better* on Saturdays?

5. Two of my new teachers, a male and a female, were in a classroom. Apparently, they had been kissing. The female had lipstick smeared all over her face. The male

Wisdom Is the *Principal* Thing!

teacher quickly went back to his desk while the female stood there, blushing. Needless to say, when I heard about it, I had to have a conversation with each of them about boundaries in the workplace!

6. The secretary calls the principal on the radio and asks him a question. He doesn't answer. She keeps calling him and asking the same question. Finally, the principal responds, "Yes, Ms. Pixy?" She asks the question yet again. There is silence on the radio. She calls him again, "Mr. Keys!" He finally snaps, "I'm thinking!" She pauses for a moment and quips, "Well, that's a good sign!"

7. A student was sent to my office with a referral for sticking his middle finger up at the teacher. We were in the middle of an accreditation team visit and the team was working out of the large conference room next to my office. The student gave me the referral and sat down. Before I could begin questioning him, one of the visitation team members stuck her head through the door of my office and said, "There's hardly any

298

more coffee in the pot." I looked at the student. The student looked at me. I looked back at the visitor and thought to myself, *Talk about being torn between priorities!*

8. I was walking down the hall of the school, and I saw this student obviously not in a place where he should be and not doing what he should be doing. As a newly hired assistant principal, I immediately went to do my job. I talked to him about policies, procedures, and acceptable behavior. I was definitely letting him know I was in charge, and I was not going to have it! I was in my "administrative" zone, and it was important for him to know that he couldn't pull the wool over *my* eyes! He stood quietly and very attentively while I lectured. When I finally paused to catch my breath, I saw the message on his T-Shirt: "Beam me up, Scottie. There's no intelligent life down here."

Find the humor: It will do you good!

ABOUT THE AUTHOR

Dr. Kathy P. Hall, formerly a teacher and assistant principal, pioneered as one of the *first* Black, newly appointed principals to open a new school in Charlotte-Mecklenburg Schools in North Carolina. Three years later, as a district office administrator, she led Charlotte-Mecklenburg Schools' truancy and dropout prevention efforts by successfully implementing several effective programs that reduced the rate of school truancy and dropouts. She also worked in Rock Hill Schools' York County District in South Carolina. Upon retiring, she founded *Hall's Consulting and Publishing Ent.*, focusing on writing, publishing, and motivational speaking.

She has an MAED in English and Administration from the University of North Carolina at Charlotte and has a doctorate in Christian Education and Leadership from Logos University in Jacksonville, Florida. As part of her business goals, she contracted with Central Piedmont Community College (CPCC) and taught writing and research methods to students.

Kathy has presented for churches, schools, and non-profit organizations, and she seeks ways to help others prosper in their personal and professional endeavors. She currently resides in the Mountain Island Lake area

Wisdom Is the *Principal* Thing!

of North Carolina with her husband, Trent. She has three adult children, Breece, Bradley and Whitney, one daughter-in-law, Crystal, and five grandsons. Kathy's philosophy of life is based on Micah 6:8 of the Bible as she often states, "God only requires three things of us, which are to be just, love mercy and walk humbly with Him."

A children's book by Kathy,
The Wise King's Christmas, is on Amazon.com
and Barnes and Noble websites.

www.ingramcontent.com/pod-product-compliance
Lightning Source LLC
Chambersburg PA
CBHW070531010526
44118CB00012B/1101